Kindness WINS

GALIT BREEN

Kindness Wins
Copyright 2015 Galit Breen

Formatting and Cover by R.A. Mizer of ShoutLines Design.

Editing by Bethany Root

Copy Editing by Tricia Parker

Book Managing by Pam Labbe

ISBN-13: 978-1533623416
ISBN-10: 1533623414

Dedication

To Jason, Kayli, Chloe, Brody, Louie, and Parker.

You are my sunshine.

PRAISE FOR *KINDNESS WINS*

"An indispensable 21st-century manual of manners written for 21st-century parents and their children. With compassion, humor, insight, and practical wisdom born of firsthand experience, Galit Breen makes a compelling case for online decency. What would happen if parents and kids everywhere could read these 10 simple rules of conduct, learn them by heart, and live by them each and every time they log in? The world would change dramatically—and for the good of us all."

—Katrina Kenison, author of *Mitten Strings for God* and *The Gift of an Ordinary Day*

———

"Thought-provoking, inspiring, and simple to grasp, *Kindness Wins* is an invaluable parenting tool filled with extremely effective ways to teach our kids how to be kind online. Simply put, when kindness wins, we all do."

—Sheila McCraith, author of *Yell Less, Love More*

———

"Engaging and accessible, *Kindness Wins* is a straightforward and nonjudgmental launching pad to help you and your children discuss how best to navigate the murky social media waters."

—Kimberly McCreight, *New York Times* best-selling author of *Reconstructing Amelia*

———

"It's not just about cyberbullying, it's about how we treat each other. Galit Breen is not only a brilliant author, she is someone who felt the pain of cyber-bullets and rose above to make a difference for others. Changing the conversation offline will help your children have healthier experiences online. This is why *Kindness Wins* is a must-read for all parents who have kids who use social media."

—Sue Scheff, Family Internet Safety Advocate

"An absolute must-read for anyone raising a child in this unfamiliar (and slightly terrifying) age of social media. I'm a better parent having read it."

—Jill Smokler, *New York Times* best-selling author of *Confessions of a Scary Mommy*

———

"Part guidebook, part conversation, *Kindness Wins* powerfully captures the essence and importance of helping our kids be kind online."

—Marcelle Soviero, Editor-in-Chief, *Brain, Child: The Magazine for Thinking Mothers*

———

"Galit Breen has written a unique, timely, and beneficial guide to bringing digital kindness to our lives and the lives of our children. Through engaging real-life examples and encouraging prose, Galit offers 10 practical guidelines that will promote healthy, intentional, and considerate habits that could help you or a loved one avoid pain and problems in both the real and online world. Galit lovingly reminds us that what we say matters—and a screen does not change that. *Kindness Wins* shows us that we have the ability to build or break ... hurt or help ... add or diminish with the click of a button. The choice is ours."

—Rachel Macy Stafford, *New York Times* best-selling author of *Hands Free Mama*

Table of Contents

Prologue

"I always wondered why somebody doesn't do something about that. Then I realized I was somebody."
— Lily Tomlin

Dear New Friend,

I knew I wanted to take a stand against cyberbullying the first time I witnessed it. I was reading a blog, scanning the comments and readying to add my own, when I noticed that one of the comments had an awful lot of exclamation points and uppercase letters in it. The words screamed, "Read me," so I did.

As I took in bits and pieces of what this commenter had to say, my heart drummed, my cheeks burned, and my fingers froze.

The comment wasn't about the blog content or topic. It was one insult layered upon another meant to do … I wasn't exactly sure what? I left the blogger a note of support so she'd know I was there for her and clicked away from the page.

Days later, I checked in on her via e-mail.

Everything okay with your crazy commenter? I asked.

Trolls. She wrote back. *What can you do?*

Since then, I've had variations of the same conversation too many times with too many people. While Internet trolls are commonplace enough to warrant an Urban Dictionary definition—"trolls are people who purposely and deliberately start arguments in ways that attack others"—all brands of cyberbullying seem to have become shrug-worthy, *it is what it is*, everyday experiences. But instead of making me shrug, cyberbullying still makes me cringe, and it still makes me want to do something to increase positivity online.

What I haven't known until recently is what that "something" could possibly be.

When my daughter gently nudged my husband, Jason, and me and said that she'd sure like to share photos on Instagram, pin, post, and tweet, my gut instinct was to say, "Yes."

Despite my occasional brush with cyberbullying, I love social media. I love the connectivity it provides, the creativity it allows, and the breathtaking wealth of information we all have at our fingertips because of it.

So I wanted to give her an Instagram account right then and there.

It was late. We were talking across the kitchen counter, beneath an evening light, with only the pull of school the next day whispering, "No."

She seemed so excited and, truly, so was I. I imagined teaching her how to use filters and editing tools, clicking the little heart beneath all of her photos, and gaining insight into her friends and their online interactions.

It ended up being that last part that gave me pause.

Many families in our town must have been having similar conversations, because once I looked for them, I quickly found social media accounts belonging to kids I knew. And from these, I learned quite a bit.

The pretty bow I can wrap around that learning is this: There's a ridiculous amount of topics to cover, teach, and explain to kids—and even some adults—before they can navigate wisely online. While I truly think that kids and adults are instinctively good, I also believe that we don't all automatically know how to use social media kindly.

So with that, I found my "something," and I wrote this book covering ten habits to directly teach kids about how to be kind online.

That might sound like a lot of (overwhelming) information. But taking the time to learn and teach online kindness now means less work later.

After reading this book and discussing it with your children, you'll be able to loosen your grip on worrying about how your kids act online, because you'll know that you've already done the hard work, had the tricky conversations, and taught them well.

I'm in this with you because we all benefit when our kids treat each other kindly and when you and I are kind to each other. In order for kindness to win we need to work together to create a new path. One where online kindness is the clear, obvious, and obstacle-free way to go. One where cyberbullying incites anything but a shrug from all of us.

The only way for us to get there is to discuss exactly how we'll do that.

So let's get started.

Galit

Introduction

"We have the potential to help people out of poverty, out of disease, out of slavery, and out of conflict. Too often, we turn the other way because we think there's nothing we can do."
— Alicia Keys

I'm a writer and a mother and a teacher, and I'm madly in love with social media. I wrote this book to connect the dots between these four puzzle pieces.

I think it's wildly important to have direct conversations about how to act kindly online. So it's my hope that what you read here will spark discussions between you and your kids and between you and your peers. Both of these conversations are equally important.

Education is our path to change. Minds and hearts are brightened via learning. And our kids—my goodness, our kids—are flexible learners who soak up information so very quickly. But the other side of this coin—the conversations we need to have with our peers—is just as valuable. Let me explain why.

Jason and I have been parenting with the same group of moms and dads for what is—in parenting years—a very long time. We watched our same-aged girls pick grass as kindergarten soccer players. We gave each other wary high-fives for making it through another class party, field trip, or volunteer "opportunity." We analyzed their test scores, organized their car pools, and wondered how the twists and turns of their friendships would work themselves out.

What's recently changed between us is that we've traded our well-worn worries about reading levels and sports choices for new frets about cell phones and Instagram accounts. Guiding our kids' social media use is a new terrain for all of us; we're muddling through, and we aren't afraid to tell each other so. Because the only thing any of us really and truly know for sure is that we're all doing our best.

Through the years, we haven't always agreed on what best parenting practices look like. And our discussions about social media aren't any different. Among us are the Instagram account checkers, the "let them be" sayers, and the "they're too young to be online" believers. Every family, parent, and tween is different, so it makes sense—and it doesn't matter—that we advocate for different parenting choices. Just like years ago it didn't matter if we unanimously decided whether or not our daughters should continue playing soccer. What has mattered in all of these situations is that we have been willing to take the time to talk to and support each other, to be open and vulnerable.

We all do parenting better when we share what we know. I've reaped these benefits firsthand. When all of our daughters were younger, we parents would settle on the edge of the soccer field side by side to cheer for our girls. Their clunky cleats and knobby knees gave away their age, and their approach to the game revealed their nature.

One golden fall night, the kind where the air sits in the soft slip between summer and autumn, and the red of the sky kisses the green of the grass, all but one of the girls

GALIT BREEN

were chasing the ball, aiming to get a goal. The lone girl, my
girl, was grasping at dandelions, bringing them close to her
lips, and making wishes, her ponytail glinting in the sunlight.
She was lovely, but she wasn't playing the game. The mom I
was sitting next to followed my heartbeat-too-long glance at
my flower-picking girl, leaned over her lawn chair, crossed
her yoga-pants-wearing legs, lifted her sunglasses with one
chipped-manicured hand, touched my arm with the other,
and said, "She'll be fine."

Not too far from where we sat, Jason stood next to
one of the dads, arms crossed and eyes on the field, mirror
images of each other. When our daughter was comparing
jersey numbers with an opposing player, Jason joked about
her team spirit and our friend reassured him that this was
completely normal for their age group. In his own way, this
father was telling Jason the exact same thing this mother was
telling me. *She'll be fine.* Today, both Jason and I understand
this clearly and gulp in the fleeting sweetness of a
kindergarten soccer game. But at the time, we needed to be
told, and to hear, that our girl was okay, that this soccer
game didn't matter all that much.

Both of these parents' messages were twofold. The
first one, the one that I breathed in that day, was that our
kids are lovely just as they are. That lesson was vital. But the
second one, the one that revolves around how to support
each other as parents, is equally important. That lesson took
me a bit longer to internalize, but today I understand that
these two been-there-done-that parents were letting us know
that, as parents, we're meant to help each other out and
build each other up. One way we can do this is by talking
openly and transparently about our parenting—how we're
feeling, what we're seeing, and what we're doing.

Social media has made this even more possible, widening our circle of available yoga-pants-clad moms and sunglasses-wearing dads to discuss the tricky parts of parenting. And this book works in the exact same way. It's meant to be the circle widener and the conversation starter.

When you're finished reading *Kindness Wins*, you'll know what I've learned as a social media enthusiast about how to act kindly online and, maybe even more importantly, you'll know what I've learned as an educator about how to teach someone else to do the same.

Becoming Social Media Savvy Is a Skill That Can Be Taught

Most of us spend a significant amount of time connected to our devices, and our kids see that. It's hard to explain to them that social media isn't relevant to their lives, because it truly is.

When I felt ready to dig into these conversations with my daughter, I asked if her teachers had discussed how to act kindly online. I wanted to build on what she already knew and use the foundation that her teachers had already laid.

But her answer surprised me. She said, "No." She actually tilted her head and scrunched her nose and pursed her lips just the right amount to let me know that my question didn't make sense to her.

So she knows what to do if she needs to evacuate a building, a bus, or a playground. This is something she's been practicing with her classmates several times a year, every year, but has (thankfully) never had to use. But she doesn't know how to maneuver through an online world that, like it or not, is already a part of her everyday life.

With every fiber of my being, I believe that our children are fundamentally good. I thought this when mine shrieked through the witching hours as infants. I vowed it when they arched their backs to protest being put in their car seats as toddlers. And when they hit or pushed or pinched as preschoolers, even then, I—perhaps grudgingly, but still—knew that their goodness reigned true.

But just like our kids had to learn how to walk, talk, read, draw, and ride their bikes, they also needed to learn how to use their voices and bodies and hands gently— kindly, if you will—and you and I had to learn how to teach them all of the above. So the good news is that we already know that our kids have the capacity to learn from us and that we have the ability to teach them; teaching our kids how to be kind online is completely within all of our skill sets.

The other piece of good news is that there's a simple formula that works to effectively teach someone just about anything and this is it: short, repeated, direct lessons, followed by modeling and the chance to try, make mistakes, and try again, all bookended with check-ins and gentle reminders. This is the best way to teach everything, online kindness included.

The truth is that you already know this formula. You used it when you taught your kids everything from writing their names to riding their bikes. In this book I'll show you how to use it when it comes to teaching online kindness.

Kindness Wins—in Person and Online

There's a secret to acting appropriately and ethically online and it's called Kindness Wins.

KINDNESS WINS

Merriam-Webster's Dictionary defines ethics as, "the rules of behavior based on ideas about what is morally good and bad."

We know what good and bad look like in person:

Opening the door for someone is good.

Closing the door in someone's face is bad.

Calling someone pretty, smart, or strong is good.

Calling someone dumb, ugly, or weak is bad.

Saying hello is good.

Ignoring is bad.

Kindness works in pretty much the exact same ways online.

I have a theory that deep down inside, just like we're all inherently good, we also already know what's right. But sometimes this knowing gets muddled. Our online lives start with peeking at people from behind the safety net of an edited and filtered avatar, which can make it even harder to remember what we all know to be true: Kindness Wins.

It just does. We treat people with kindness because it's the right thing to do. It's why we open doors and carry boxes for people, and it's why we say thank you and give compliments. It's also exactly why we should interact and comment and reply with kindness online.

Author and speaker Dennis Prager wrote, "Goodness is about character, integrity, honesty, kindness, generosity, moral courage, and the like. More than anything else, it is about how we treat other people."

This definition of goodness being wrapped up in how we treat others is what it all comes down to—in person and online.

When I write online, the second my editor or I hit *Publish*, we give the power to readers, and they have to decide how to respond.

Sometimes, people are kind. I've been told by online commenters that I'm pretty, smart, and strong.

And sometimes, people are cruel. I've also been told that I'm dumb, ugly, and weak.

I wrote this book after Jason and I ended up on the *Today* show and *Inside Edition* because people, many people actually, saw our wedding photos online and commented how fat I looked in the pictures.

In this book, I explain what happened in that situation —how kindness still won even in such a gross display of meanness, and what all of this has to do with you. I'm going to start with that last one.

Online Kindness Begins with You

Author Katrina Kenison says that we're living in world with a kindness deficit. My experience tells me she's right. I saw and felt cyberbullying firsthand. But I also found a ridiculous amount of kindness and like-minded people who knew, like you know and I know, that we can't go on allowing our kids, ourselves, and each other to maneuver online without a kindness filter.

There's a better way, and I think we can all do—and be—better than that.

We can step over the *people are free to say whatever they want* stumbling block with gentle teaching and re-teaching that free speech isn't a license to be cruel. Nothing is.

We can flip our thinking from competitive parenting to parenting together in order to give all of our kids all of our best by watching out for each other and each other's children.

We can create an online space where we feel comfortable letting our tweens and teens maneuver and

11

learn and utilize the amazing (and fun) tools available to them by teaching them how to do all of the above kindly.

Such change is possible and it's where *Kindness Wins* comes in. This book is made for anyone and everyone you know who is online, especially if you have kids and you buy their phones or give them Internet access.

In these pages I'll explain ten online habits to teach and model, covering photos, comments, shares, tags, and even debates about tough, sensitive topics. At the end of each section, you'll find one resource for further reading, two discussion starters—one to use with kids and one to use with peers—and three bulleted takeaways that summarize what you just read.

After reading these ten rules, you'll have the chance to commit to what you've learned by using the two *Kindness Wins* contracts at the end of the book.

The first contract is between you and your peers. I want you to agree to look out for each other and each other's children. We can be each other's village. All of us—and our kids—will be better for it.

And the second contract is between you and the child you're trying to teach how to act kindly online. This contract isn't about when to turn off the phone or who will pay for what, although these are important topics that should be negotiated and discussed. The heart of this contract lies in how to approach social media use. Be kind or don't go online. The end.

Actually, once upon a time.

Once upon a time, the biggest mistake your child could make was to not put away her toys or to draw on the kitchen table. Today, she's a little bit older and you might be thinking that she'd never act meanly online. Let's discuss that next.

Chapter 1

"Not My Kid" Is Simply Not True

"Success does not consist in never making mistakes but in never making the same one a second time."
— George Bernard Shaw

When I was thirteen years old, my friend and I snuck out of my house after dark to meet boys at the baseball field. The walk was long and the night was rainy. We weren't wearing jackets, because when you're thirteen and hanging out with the kind of friend who makes your side hurt from laughing, jackets aren't on your mind.

We walked to and from that field arm in arm, our words whipping over each other, braiding our friendship tightly.

When we got back to my house, our hair and our clothes and our shoes were soaked. We unlocked the door, still laughing and talking, and looked away from each other, straight into my father's eyes.

We all stood still for a heartbeat, water dripping to the floor between my friend and me in the seemingly slow motion that happens when you know you've done something wrong and your parents are silent about it. Finally, he asked, "What were you doing?"

My dad, tall and serious with piercing blue eyes and a Russian accent that would silence my future husband mid-sentence, was giving me a lifeline.

I could have told the truth. I could have said we went outside. We were on a walk. We were doing something—anything—that could have resulted in two soaked-from-head-to-toe girls. But, no. I didn't think of any of these ideas.

"We did each other's hair," is what I (weakly) said.

My dad's eyes flashed, assessing all the ways he knew I was lying, starting, of course, with the front door we had just walked through.

My parents had never sat me down to discuss the dangers of sneaking out after dark and of not letting anyone know where I was—not to mention the lack of wisdom in leaving their home unlocked. They assumed, with good reason, that I knew better. I was a good kid with nice friends. I was polite to grown-ups and respectful of teachers. I did my chores and I got good grades. And yet, here I was, caught in the act of sneaking out (and back in!), forcing my parents to have the "no sneaking out" discussion with me the next day.

While I definitely believe in and strive to live by Shaw's words that introduce this chapter, I know—from unfortunate experience—that we make some mistakes several times before we learn the lessons from them.

And, most importantly, I know that we need to directly teach our children the most vital lessons, rather than assume that they'll be understood.

I believe the same is true with social media. Although days of sneaking out without having phones in hand are

14

long gone, muddling through being a kid, and being a parent, is still pretty much the same.

What's different is the addition of technology and social media.

When my son was two years old, he walked up to a screen and swiped it.

When my daughter was five, she started a DVD via the Xbox for me.

And when my oldest daughter was ten, she knew how to pin on Pinterest and asked questions like, "Are you posting that?"

Our kids are savvy and incredibly lucky to have these amazing tools at their tiny fingertips. I don't begrudge them this and think it would be a disservice to not let them be online. I believe this is true for two reasons.

The first is that having an online presence is the reality of the time we live in, and they'll need to be social media savvy for current school and future work opportunities. And the second reason, the one that's more focused on the present moment, is that social media is one way kids are connecting with each other. And taking away an opportunity for connecting and relationship forming isn't our job as parents. Teaching our kids how to do this responsibly and kindly is.

So it's that "tiny fingertips" part that I want to hone in on—they're still kids. And even though they've grown up with technology as a part of their daily lives, they will make mistakes while using it.

This means that we need to have direct conversations with our kids about the kinds of comments that are okay to make. It's showing them an appropriate comment and an inappropriate one and having the discussion with them about what makes one okay and the other not.

KINDNESS WINS

When we were young and a friend did something that bothered us, we went about our lives, going to sports practice, having dinner with our family, doing our homework, and then—if we had time and still remembered —we called our friend (or sometimes, someone else) to tell them what had happened and why we were upset.

Kids today have a phone tucked inside their thumb-holed sleeves, and if someone bothers them or they're in a bad mood or their feelings are hurt or their hormones are high, they can text, comment, or message their angst instantly without taking the time to cool down.

This can be costly for even the kindest of kids. I shudder when thinking about the decisions I'd make and the words I'd blurt if I didn't use a thoughts-to-actions filter. Our kids are definitely still developing the skills of taking deep breaths and thinking through their actions, but the availability and immediacy of technology makes it difficult for them to practice.

We need to teach them to take a breath before they post online, just like we teach them to take a breath before they talk back to us, a teacher, a coach, or a friend.

We need to teach them that not every status needs to be commented on. That not every thought needs to be shared. That not every event needs to be documented.

We need to teach them that it's okay to walk away sometimes, and how to step into and out of a situation as necessary.

And we need to teach them how to come back from the missteps they will take, and how to apologize.

Just like even the nicest of kids will make mistakes, even the savviest of parents won't be able to keep tabs on everything their kids do on (and off!) line. Texts can be deleted. Search histories can be cleared. And friends can be muted online.

We can't assume that because we check their phones we don't need to teach our kids how to act kindly online. We can't—and shouldn't—parent like we'll always be there to catch them, because in reality we won't. Instead, we can teach them how to maneuver kindly online on their own.

Once we taught our kids how to walk, we could trust them to know how to walk anywhere (within reason!). We could exhale our worries away. This teaching works in the exact same way.

1 Resource:

"Should We Talk to Young Children about Race?" by Rodolfo Mendoza-Denton on *GreaterGood.com* is a smartly written article explaining why brain-based researchers and *Nurture Shock* authors Po Bronson and Ashley Merryman advocate directly talking to kids about important topics. Our kids are always maneuvering, learning, and assuming. It's our job to provide them with the framework for how to do all of the above deftly.

2 Things to Talk About:

Discuss with Your Kids

The best way to help our kids learn how to maneuver kindly online is to give them a chance to practice doing so—repeatedly and with real examples.

13 likes

purplefuzzysocks Selfie time!

princessdiamondtiara ur fat! go on a diet!

butterfreeichooseu ur so cool!! ^_^

soccorbug22 yaay purple!

carl_the_creeper uglly! delete this ugly pic!

soccorbug22 ur SO mean carl!

carl_the_creeper shut up, soccorbug! u have a dumb name!

Example: Photo Comments

Sit down with your kids and show them an example of a status or a photo with comments on it, like the one that follows.

Look at posts such as this one and see if your child can pinpoint comments that are okay to make—the ones that do no harm—and the ones that aren't okay. You and I may not agree on which comments fall under the "okay" category and which ones are "not okay." This is just fine. The important part here is the dialogues we'll each have with our kids and the think-before-you-post habits these conversations will instill in them.

Repeat this regularly with different threads. We wouldn't give our kids one driving lesson, hand them the keys, and send them on their way with crossed fingers and a "good luck." We'd let them practice, learn, make mistakes, and try again. The same process applies here. So in your revisiting-the-topic conversations, you can choose to formally sit down together or to share examples in passing.

Here's what I mean by that. My second favorite place in the world, trumped only by my bed, is our yellow couch. I often decompress on that couch with a book if I want time to myself, or with my phone if I want to see what everyone else is up to. Almost daily, my daughter flops down next to me, starts reading over my shoulder, and says, "What are you doing?" It can be awfully tempting to say, "Nothing," because, after all, I'm relaxing. What I'm doing probably isn't important or relevant to her. Except that, in some cases, it is.

Moments like these are golden opportunities to meld what I'm seeing online with what she needs to know, so when she's scrolling through Facebook, Twitter, or

Instagram, she has a framework for what scrolling kindly looks and feels like.

So when she asks what I'm doing, I grasp the opportunity and show her an example. If she overhears Jason and me discussing something we saw online and asks what we're talking about, we tell her. We bring her into the conversation and step into the teachable moment.

Sometimes, I take the initiative to bring up examples when I'm talking to her. If she's ready to be online, she's ready for these conversations. And if I'm ready to hand her a phone, I have to be ready for them, too.

We all learn better with repeated small lessons. We can use this to our advantage and keep these dialogues short and open.

Discuss with Your Peers

There are two things to discuss with our peers who may believe they don't have to monitor their kids' social media use. The first is that all kids are capable of making mistakes, and the second is that all adults are, too.

With our peers—the ones we parent with, the ones who know and (possibly) love our kids—we can discuss how we'll watch out for each other's children. What will we share if we see them acting inappropriately or dangerously online?

Will we be online with our kids? Will we follow their Instagram accounts or friend them on Facebook? I'm a firm "yes" in both of these cases. And if my kids' friends follow me, I follow them back. Here's why.

The kids who follow the grown-ups they know on social media aren't the kids I'm worried about. They don't see their online lives as something they need to hide or be sneaky about. They're the kids I care about and I want to

20

support and see shine. I think we all feel this way about each other's children. They're fun to cheer on.

The only downfall to following and friending our kids and their friends on social media is that this may mean thinking twice about what we post ourselves, because our tweens and teens will now see it. But the truth is they can Google our accounts at any time and, apparently, they do like to do this.

I found this out at a gathering at a friend's house. With a cocktail in one hand and an appetizer in the other, I suddenly heard the buzz that could only mean one thing: the kids had come into the room. I heard my name and my husband's name as well, so I (curiously) turned around to see what they were up to.

What I saw was all of our kids gathered around the family laptop Googling the adults' names. They stood shoulder to shoulder like stair steps, and while I could only see them from behind, I could hear their excitement from where I stood. It was palpable. "There's your mom!" I heard one girl say to mine as they turned toward each other. I could see their faces in profile, their cheeks lifted and their eyes bright. In this case, they were doing this innocently and purely for fun.

But there I was for them to see. All of us adults were. Our photos and our social media links were lined up and ready to be clicked, taking them right to our profiles. So if our kids are going to see our accounts anyway, we might as well embrace the situation and act as if they're watching.

The truth is that we're their examples for appropriate —kind—behavior, offline and online. So we shouldn't hide our feeds from them. Instead, we should model the openness we'd like our tweens to mirror.

Another truth is that teaching and modeling kindness is a privilege, and we're lucky to be the ones to get to do it. The benefits of being informed about our kids' online lives and of seeing how they interact with their friends and their acquaintances online far outweigh the inconvenience of being mindful of what we post.

The second part of this discussion with peers, the one that may be harder to swallow, is that we need to think about what we'll say or do if it's one of our friends who's acting unkindly online.

We're modeling the behavior we want to see. The way we act online should match the way we act in person. So if an adult we know posts something insensitive, how do we bring it up to him or her? What will we say? Will it be in person or over the phone or in a private message? In Chapters 3 and 8, I share times when people did this for me, detailing what they said that made the conversations so very effective.

We ask a lot of our kids. We tell them to stand up and be a source of positive change when they see, hear, or do something that isn't right. I'm gently suggesting that we ask the same of ourselves.

3 Takeaways:

- Every kid is capable of making a mistake online.
- Checking our kids' social media outlets isn't the same thing as teaching them how to use these channels kindly.
- Directly teaching—with real examples—is the best way to explain what's okay to say and do online and what's not.

Chapter 2

Remember There's Someone on the Other Side of the Screen

"I've learned that people will forget what you said, people will forget what you did, but people will never forget how you made them feel."
— Dr. Maya Angelou

My parents and I used to go to a resort in Canada for one week every summer. We'd spend mornings on the docks, days at the lake, and nights in the front hall with the other families who were there that week.

The mix of people was eclectic and I loved it. The family of four with their name-brand swimsuits who stayed during the same week and in the same cabin every single year. The couple who paid me two dollars to watch their new baby while they went for a swim or a walk. And the family who always seemed to have an extra kid to play with, splash with, and spend time with.

The people who worked there were local kids with summer jobs. Their tan lines were defined and their inside jokes were solid. They were the constants; we were the unknowns.

They were the lifeguards and the art directors and the tennis instructors, and in my young eyes they couldn't possibly have been cooler.

One summer, one of these cool teens took me under her wing. She invited me to eat lunch with her under the big tree, shared her sunscreen, and showed me the best rock to jump into the lake from.

I don't remember her name or what color her hair was, but I do remember how nice she was to me and that she made me feel like she wanted me to be there, but not just because it was her job to be nice to all of the vacationing kids.

These are the things that people remember. This is true in real life, on vacation, and online.

In the previous section we agreed that even the most well-behaved, nicest kids—and adults—are capable of making mistakes and would benefit from direct lessons in how to maneuver online kindly. In this chapter I want to dive into the conversation that is at the base of all the others that follow: When it comes to teaching online kindness, the best place to start is teaching that there's someone on the other side of our comments and our actions.

When we text and comment and "like"—and don't "like"—it's easy to forget this, because we can't see reactions to our actions.

There isn't a smile over lunch beneath a big tree to show that we've done something right. And there isn't a hurt look or a teary eye or a shaky voice to show that we've done something wrong, that we've hurt someone.

Without these social cues, we have to understand the concept of the ripples we create with our actions—before we're given Internet reign.

The "good" news is that it's not difficult to figure out if something's unkind online. The actions that hurt people's feelings in person—mean words and being left out—are the exact same ones that hurt people's feelings online.

We've already been teaching our kids these unwritten social rules for a long time. "Be nice," "Ask her to play," and "Don't talk about the party at school" have been part of our parenting and socialization arsenal for many, many years. Now we just need to translate these to our online lessons. We can do that by looking at real posts and discussing how different people may view—and feel about—them.

Example: Best Friends List

One of the creative things kids do to personalize their profile pages is to list who their best friends are, like in this example.

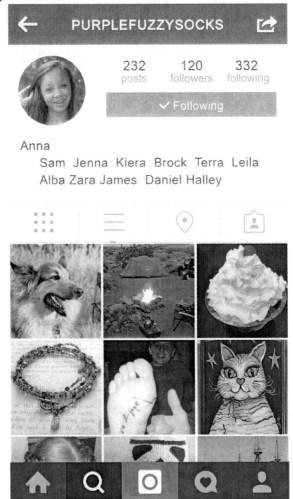

This makes perfect sense as tweens and teens are starting to redefine who they are based on their friendships. Author and speaker Jim Rohn says, "You are the average of the five people you spend the most time with." I love this concept and believe in it.

But when I looked at some tweens' and teens' profiles —nice kids with technologically savvy parents—I saw clues indicating that, when turned around and looked at from another perspective, best friend listing can be done or taken unkindly.

The first clue were comments like this: *But I thought I was your best friend?*

The second was the *now you see it, now you don't* phenomenon of a best friend being listed one day and deleted the next.

In this same vein, kids are posting photos labeled with "Tag Your Squad" or "Tag Your 15 Favorite People." What I told my daughter about these kinds of games is that if she plays, she should tag everyone who follows her or not participate.

I also told her that's exactly what *I* do when I get tagged in photos like these. I shared this with her because there are two important messages I want to send to my kids about their social media use. The first is that they never have to participate in anything online that they don't want to. And the second is that anything that might hurt someone's feelings should fall into the "don't want to" category.

purplefuzzysocks

♥ sherlock_domes, amber_reid, yes_fn_maam

● purplefuzzysocks if you don't want them,
tag them
matt_schuster amber_reid
amber_reid r u serious?? :'(

Example: "Tag Who You Want Out"

There are also games kids play in their feeds. Posting photo collages of their friends and asking their followers to tag who they want to "vote out" is one example.

Sometimes kids do this without posting the photo collage. A harmless-looking photo of a craft or a scene or a selfie is paired with a list of names and an ask to tag who you want out and perhaps a "good luck." Parents scrolling through feeds without clicking into the photos and reading the words would never know this was going on.

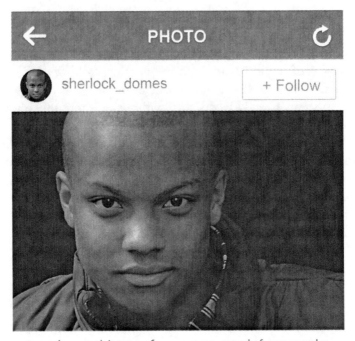

PHOTO

sherlock_domes

+ Follow

♥ amber_reid, yes_fn_maam, purplefuzzysocks

sherlock_domes
#rate #rateme #ratemehot #ratemeplease #ratei

purplefuzzysocks 7 ♥♥♥

yes_fn_maam 10/10! woo!

amanda_reid 2 :/

winter_rose big fat zeroooooo!

kaylaamanda 6 ☺

Example: #RateMePlease

Another trend is to ask your followers to rate your looks. Some kids hashtag these photos so strangers—Instagram users whom they don't follow and who don't follow them—can search Instagram by these hashtags, find their photos, and rate them.

Today, when I searched Instagram for these hashtags, this is how many photos were tagged with them:

> #rateme 220,269 posts
> #ratemehot 1,707 posts
> #ratemeplz 1,299 posts
> #ratemeplease 1,090 posts

I'm not sure that anyone needs so much input online, so I tell my kids to not ask for this kind of feedback and to not participate if one of their friends does. Your family might decide differently. The value is in the conversations we have, not the (personal) decisions we make. And #rateme is amazing dialogue fodder. We can begin conversations about why kids—and adults—might participate in this and how they may feel depending on the feedback they get. Sometimes even positive feedback garners negative emotions.

This is a great opportunity to discuss internal and external validation and how both have their place and value.

KINDNESS WINS

232
posts

120
followers

332
following

✓ Following

The Matchmaker
Follow for your match!!
Shutouts accepted. <3

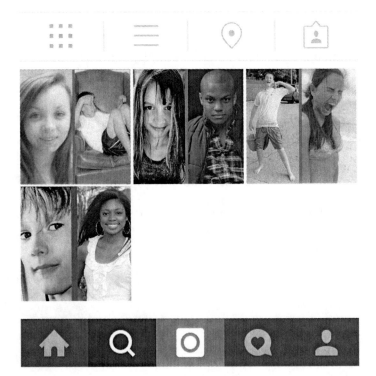

Example: Matchmaker, Matchmaker

Another game kids play on social media is creating anonymous profiles with the purpose of matching up unknowing peers as couples.

Kids in this age group have strong personalities, senses of humor, and a general with-it-ness about the world that are both exciting and inspiring. Their newfound sarcasm—and occasional mood swings!—might make their hearts seem tough, but they're really not. With growth and change comes vulnerability. Games like these can play on insecurities and can really hurt feelings.

Kids who are feeling vulnerable or insecure—or even just impulsive—might respond defensively to being matched up with a peer. Defensive posts are rarely kind. I've seen written responses ranging from *um, no* and *redo* to *never* and *eeww gross*.

Some of these games and posts aren't outwardly mean or easy to spot as problematic. And the truth is, they're not going to be hurtful to every kid. Our kids are unique and will respond differently to being included—or excluded—from these kinds of posts.

But when you turn these posts and comments around and look at them from someone else's point of view—from the perspective of the deleted best friend or the voted-out girl—you can see why they might be hurtful. So rather than making specific decisions about whether or not our kids should participate in these kinds of posts, it's more important to teach them to practice the habit of "turning them around."

Do you remember the heart-stopping scene in *The Breakfast Club* when Andrew Clark, the stereotypical jock played by Emilio Estevez, realized that after he taped Larry

Lester's butt cheeks together, Lester had to go home and tell his dad what had happened? The same story would sound awfully different when told by Clark rather than Lester. Every time I've watched this part of this beloved movie—as a teen, as a teacher, and as a mom—I've cringed because it's such a brilliantly cut-to-the-heart-of-things example of seeing something from someone else's point of view.

The concept that this scene illustrates is the same one we'll teach our kids when we help them see their posts from someone else's perspective. Teaching kids that their online actions, words, and shares can have an impact on themselves breeds responsibility. But teaching them that their online choices may affect others encourages empathy, and therefore, kindness.

The discussions we'll have with our kids will go far beyond, "Don't do that." They'll circle around intent, points of view, and ripples.

Become Aware of Unspoken Social Currency

Author and researcher Rachel Simmons documented how girls look to Instagram to see how they measure up against each other. The number of comments or "likes" a photo or a status gets is a tangible way that kids measure their popularity against each other. Tagging is another social currency.

I actually find the amount of importance kids place on the number of photos they're tagged in to be so very interesting. It takes a little bit of sleuthing to see who's tagged in photos and who's not. You have to click an extra button or go to a user's profile and click into the "person" icon to see all of the photos they've been tagged in, and even if you choose to take these steps—depending on whether or not you're following each other or how the privacy settings are set—you might not find what you're looking for.

But even though photo tags aren't blatantly right there to see, I wonder if their popularity is due to the phenomenon I call Greener Grass Perception.

Many writers have noted that when we look at others' social media feeds, we're looking at their highlight reels. We're seeing their shiny moments. The ones they're choosing to edit, filter, share, and remember. There's absolutely nothing wrong with this. Greener Grass Perception is all in the eyes of the social media pursuer, not the poster.

Even though we all know this truth, it's tempting to forget that behind highlight reels there are always bloopers. So on an emotional day or a tired day or a just plain-and-fine gray day, we compare our bloopers to others' highlights. And from that we take on Greener Grass Perception.

Perhaps this is what's happening when our kids become insecure based on the number of photos they're tagged in. They're assuming that others must have more tagged photos, and therefore have shinier, happier, and fuller lives.

This is great fodder for conversations with your kids. By (repeatedly!) bringing up the truths that everyone has highlight reels and blooper reels, you can explain that Greener Grass Perception is just that, a perception. They'll need to sit with some of their jealousy and sadness and then they'll need to practice the habit of moving forward. One of my kid's teachers used to say, "Get all the facts before you react." In this case, it might be apt to say, "Don't (over)react without the facts."

Example: Tagged Scenes

We can use these mantras to help us maneuver conversations about other kinds of tags as well. A wildly popular trend is to post a photo of a scene of a place you're at, or even one that you're not at, and to tag it with friends.

This is an especially powerful tool when the photo isn't of an actual event, and kids can see that they're tagged (included) or not (left out). Sometimes users will exclude a friend or first tag and then untag someone whom they're angry with.

Talk to your kids about this kind of post—not necessarily to make sure that they don't do this, because that's between you and your kids—but to start a dialogue. Talking about how someone else might feel if this happened to them will lead your kids to decide on their own how hurtful this specific type of post can be. They'll know if you believe it's unkind, they'll sit with the empathy they'll (be forced to) feel during your conversation, and they'll practice the habit of looking at a post from someone else's point of view.

I asked my own kids if they would feel hurt about not being tagged in photos and games on social media. Their answers (pleasantly) surprised me. They said "no," because it's not realistic to expect to be included in everything.

We'll need to find the balance between helping our kids remember that "like" and "tag" currencies don't equal their self-worth and, at the same time, acknowledging and respecting that this age group does come with insecurities that social media can exacerbate.

purplefuzzysocks

winter_rose

purplefuzzysocks

mary_perez

kaylaamanda

31 likes

purplefuzzysocks #besties #bestiesforlife #bestiesfortheresties

winter_rose xoxo

We can do this by listening to our kids talk when they're sad and by not dismissing their feelings. At a separate time, when their hearts aren't hurting, we can point out that even—perhaps especially—in the age of social media, when everyone is our "friend" or our "follower," we can't actually be a part of everything. And, importantly, that this is okay.

We can help our kids practice taking the times they're not included at face value, no inferences required. We can remind them—gently, often—that when they're not included in a photo, a tag, or an experience, to not make it a reflection of themselves or their friendships. I had a boss who always said, "The simplest answer is almost always right." Her words were a professional version of, "Keep it simple, silly." This is a great mantra to use during discussions about being included or left out. The simplest answer to why you weren't included is that it's impossible to be a part of everything.

We can teach these habits directly by saying these mantras, by modeling healthy reactions to our kids' getting-left-out experiences, and by being aware of our own reactions when we experience this with our peers.

And on the flip side of everything, we can use these discussions to help cement the empathy we're trying to build in our kids to ensure that they're thinking of others' feelings before they post—and tag.

So the goal of the conversations we'll have about tagging, inclusion, and exclusion is to raise awareness, thoughtfulness, empathy, and kindness. What each family decides to do about their kids' tagging practices is, of course, personal. What we'll all own together is agreeing to have the conversations.

Example: Counting—and Comparing —"Likes"

Counting the number of "likes" kids' photos receive might not sound like an activity that we, as parents, need to take part in. But noticing zero "likes" is.

KINDNESS WINS

Kids compare how many "likes" they get on their photos to how many "likes" their friends get. Girls will decide together to not "like" someone's photo if they're angry with that person. This is a modern-day version of not being included at the lunch table or being the last one picked for a team in gym class.

Other times the situation is less aggressive; kids just scroll past someone in the same way they would pass by that person in a school hallway. But because the photo and the "likes"—or lack thereof—are more permanent than a passing moment in school, counting photo "likes" feels like a way to measure popularity and self-worth. Let's teach our kids to notice if someone has zero likes and to fix that problem. Better yet, let's teach them to see someone being ignored or not noticed as a problem in the first place.

Example: To Be Honest Comments

To Be Honest (TBH) comments are a trend designed to let friends know what we really think about them.

20 likes

purplefuzzysocks Sunday Selfie <3

winter_rose TBH I dnt know u that well

amanda_reid TBH Beautiful!!

matt_schuster TBH eh

dantheman TBH you don't want to know lol

sherlock_domes TBH hm ... nah

kaylaamanda Love you!!!

These, too, can be used kindly or not. Discuss with your kids whether they'll post TBH comments and if so, what kind of comments they'll leave. When we each have these conversations with our kids, our goals will be different. Some of us will ask our kids to not ask for or leave TBH comments, and others might just remind our kids to only leave kind TBH comments, especially if there are already unkind ones on a post. Both of these guidelines are perfect and different at the same time. Where our goals will crisscross is where it really matters: By starting the conversation, we'll further instill the habit of considering others' feelings before we post.

1 Resource:

"The Secret Language of Girls on Instagram" by Rachel Simmons on *Time.com* is an eye-opening account and breakdown of how girls use Instagram as their modern playground. It's where plays for popularity and digs at insecurity reign. Simmons, cofounder of the Girls Leadership Institute and author of the *New York Times* best-selling book *Odd Girl Out: The Hidden Culture of Aggression in Girls*, lets parents in on the inner workings of our girls on Instagram.

2 Things to Talk About:

Discuss with Your Kids

Sit down with your kids and share posts in your own feed, review their friends' feeds, or go over the examples in this book.

Discuss the possible reactions to these posts from every perspective. One thing to note is that you won't always be able to spot troublesome online behavior with quick glances. You'll need to click on the photos your kids are posting and seeing. Read the comments. Tell your kids you'll be doing this. Better yet, do this with them and have the important conversations about what you're both seeing.

This is also the time to decide what we want to teach our kids to do when they see these types of posts on their own.

Teaching them to not post anything overtly unkind is a given.

But this is also an opportunity—a scary, uncomfortable opportunity, but an opportunity nonetheless —to discuss with our kids that there are also times to stand up and be the one to try to stop unkind behavior.

How will they do that? What will they say or type? We'll discuss these nitty-gritty details in the next chapter.

The details of what you and your kids decide is okay to post and what's not okay to post don't actually matter. It's the conversation that's valuable and that teaches the habit of considering others' feelings before posting online.

Discuss with Your Peers

One of the most important lessons I learned as a teacher, as a mom, and as a writer, is that more often than not, the best ideas come from the person next door. Don't be afraid to ask your friends how they want their kids to respond to unkindness when they see it online.

They might have answers that you love and want to replicate. Or they might have ideas that, when tweaked just a little, will work for you and your family.

Simply asking questions opens the door to working together. And once this is the case, you'll suddenly have peers to bounce ideas off of; you won't be attempting to figure all of this out on your own. Together, you'll be able to decide how much you want to tell each other when your own kids are involved. What would you want to be told about your own child—if she's the victim, the instigator, or the joiner-inner? Chances are, at one point or another she'll play each of these roles on purpose or by accident.

There's a lot going on in social media and *kids will be kids* doesn't apply here. Being a tween and teen online is a brand-new experience. None of us have been there, so we need to help each other maneuver this new parenting terrain.

After you read an article that strikes you, share it with other parents and always pass along tidbits of information to your peers when you see or hear something that's important about their kids. Figuring out how important something is can be as simple as asking yourself if it would help you parent your own kids.

We told each other about the latest thoughts on crib bumper use, BPA worries, and hot slide dangers. We shared where to go for the best swim lessons and warned just how much it hurts to step on the tiniest of Lego pieces in the middle of the night. And now, we need to tell each other about this.

3 Takeaways:

- Click into the photos and statuses in your kids' feeds. Read the comments and have the important conversations about what you're seeing.
- Teach your kids to imagine how every person involved in a post would feel when seeing it—who's tagged and who's not and why. Encourage them to post as if they're facing a person and posting *at* them.
- Every action has a reaction. And every post is meant to incite a reaction. What's the purpose of yours? If it's not kind, don't post it.

Chapter 3

Learn How to Call Each Other Out

"It takes a great deal of bravery to stand up to our
enemies, but just as much to stand up to our friends."
— J. K. Rowling

I traveled abroad my junior year of college. It took all the
gumption I had buried deep inside the crevices of my heart
to leave what I knew to be true. I had great friends, a
beautiful apartment, a wonderful major, and UC Davis, my
alma mater, was the quintessential college my heart's desires
were made of.

But deep inside, the other truth I knew for sure was
that I wanted to push my edges and make them a little less
smooth and predictable and a little more rough and authentic.
I wanted the scars that only real-life learning could provide.
So I left my safety net and I went to Israel.

Once there, I spent my days in class learning
elementary-level Hebrew. My still-unlined hands wrapped
around crisply sharpened pencils, note-taking my way to
language, culture, and learning. I spent my evenings with new
friends in new-to-me outdoor corridors and bars.

KINDNESS WINS

My in-between times were spent in the tiny on-campus apartment I shared with my Israeli roommate. I cooked in a kitchen that was so bare-bones that when we stood side by side boiling water for afternoon Nescafé, we were out of room. Our flip-flops touched and our backs hit the folding chairs surrounding the card table that served as our dining area. Stray cats wandered in and out of our apartment. The evening heat never dissipated. Our beds consisted of thin mats and scratchy sheets that ended up balled at the edge of our bare toes every single night. We fell asleep surrounded by the sounds and scents that come with open windows and plastic window fans.

And my nights were spent with my classmates building friendships so new and so magical I wanted to tuck them all away into my pocket and keep them there forever. We spent hours leaning against the concrete benches that lined our apartment-style dorms. Our shirts sticking to our backs, we drank cheap beer, played confusing card games, and talked about the world as it made sense to us. The Israelis and the Americans whom I spent my time with were all looking for the same edges that I was, and we were all crossing our fingers that we'd find them with each other.

After a day of shopping at the shuk, the open-air market, we spent a night just like this. We were telling stories of the deals we got and the ones we didn't. The beer was flowing, the laughter was loud, and we were all doing our best to outdo each other's stories. "I got gypped," I said, about a silver ring that I paid too much for and that I still have and love. Most of my friends laughed and moved on to the next story.

But one didn't. She dipped her cigarette to the side, flipped her long, curly blond hair over one bare, tanned shoulder, and, blowing smoke from the corner of her red-tinged lips, motioned for me to lean in and listen. And when I did, she talked into my ear just loud enough to be heard over our friends. "Hey," she said. "That's racist. You're stereotyping gypsies as thieves." She took another drag of her cigarette and added, "I thought you'd want to know."

I was twenty years old and as much as I traveled to learn, I was also traveling because I thought that I already knew so very much. After all, in my mind, I'd left the comfort zone, I did what was hard, and I was worldly.

But I was also wrong. And my friend did something that could have been awkward or hard or weird. But she didn't make it that way, and because she was so confident and nice and breezy about it, I followed her lead.

The truth is that this is very, very hard to do—as an adult and as a kid. My friend's ease with this conversation was an aberration. But she was also prepared. She knew what she believed in and what right and wrong sounded like to her, and she spoke up when she heard either one. We all need these kinds of clear lines, that kind of practice, and the confidence that comes with both. What we need are real words we can use when we see or hear something that isn't right.

Standing up for others is what we tell our kids to do. We also tell them that people who stand by and do nothing when someone is bullied are as bad as the person doing the bullying.

The exact same truth applies online. The owners of online magazines and open forums and Facebook and Instagram threads (and that probably includes you and me) owe it to each other, to kindness, and to ethics, to not allow people to be bullies online. When we stand by, we're allowing it, condoning it, and making it okay. Just like my friend told me to stop using a dated, offensive word on a hot night on a college campus, we can do the same thing today for the people in our social media feeds who need a gentle reminder every now and then.

But how do we do that?

Experience tells me that saying "Stop" is hard, but scrolling is easier.

Begin there. Teach your kids to not engage. Teach them that they don't want to be a part of anything hurtful. This is a good start. A very good start, even.

But an even bigger step is helping our kids come up with wording that will be easy for them to say when they have the opportunity to stand up against this kind of behavior. And the best way to do this is to start a direct conversation with them about it.

Kids need words that sound like them.

That's mean.

Not touching that.

Not cool.

Maybe. When I asked my daughters what they would say if they came across a "game" like the "Tag Who You Want Out" post we looked at earlier in this book, their thoughts were different from mine, and equally effective in defusing a negative "game" or comment thread. They flipped the conversation to a positive.

I love them all so much! <3

I can't choose, they're all GREAT!

I'll keep you all! xoxo

More often than not our kids' hearts are so very good. They know what's right and they see what's right in this world and the people in it. What they need to hear from us is that their instincts are right, their voices are worthy, and they should be heard.

Once we've practiced these kinds of responses with them, they'll be available to our kids and ready to use. They'll be on the tip of their fast-typing fingers, exactly where we want them to be.

1 Resource:

"The One Conversation That Could Save Your Teen's Life (and Your Own)" by Glennon Doyle Melton on *Momastery.com*, a personal essay written in Melton's trademark heart- and humor-filled style, is about the importance of teaching our kids what words to use in tough situations rather than leaving them floundering with the ambiguous advice to "simply" use their words.

2 Things to Talk About:

Discuss with Your Kids

Sit down with your kids and look at examples of online bullying you've come across, or use the examples in this book. Practice what they'll say (type) in response if their goal is to stop a behavior, and what they'll say (type) if they want to defuse a situation. Somebody can make a difference by standing up for kindness—why not them? Teach them to be that kid.

Really let them mull over the words and make sure they feel easy to say. If the words don't feel comfortable, chances are, they won't use them.

One of my first years of teaching, I had a student who crawled into my heart and has taken up residence there ever since. She was sweet, with a magnetic draw to kindness, as well as smart, with a quip-filled sense of humor. She'd unabashedly, and contagiously, belly laugh when our class read the antics of *Junie B. Jones* together. But I would just as often catch glimpses of her getting a titch teary when I was reading E. B. White's words out loud. She was a heart gem.

I was a new-ish teacher, and while I saw every bit of her goodness, I missed a bit of her smarts, and the math I was assigning was too easy for her.

One morning while I was readying for the day, with lesson plans and sharpened pencils and readied projects piled (much too) high on my (much too) small desk, I saw that I had an e-mail from this student's mom. She'd devised a plan with her daughter to address this math issue with me. Her daughter came up with the idea to complete that day's assignment and bring it directly to me instead of turning it into the "Work" basket as had become our class's routine. When she handed me her work, she planned to say, "I finished my math. It was easy for me. May I try something else?" Her mom was writing to let me know that the conversation was coming. She was setting both of us up for success.

In the years that have passed since then, I've recounted the fabulous parenting that happened in this situation and used it as a model and a reminder for how I want to advocate for my own kids. This sweet student of mine received a million good messages from her mom, starting with, "You can be the one to stand up and create change," and ending with, "Anything can be said well if practiced."

This is exactly what I want us to do with our kids. Help them practice the words they'll use, so when they need them, they'll be available to them.

I also think it's worthy to discuss with our kids how they'll tell us if they see something troublesome in their feeds, and what they'll want from us when they do come to us.

They might want our help dissecting what to say, but they might just want us to listen, and whenever possible we'll need to respect their wishes. It's our privilege to have them come to us. We need to act like it.

Discuss with Your Peers

We have to decide with our friends what we will tell each other about what we see in our kids' online behavior and, equally importantly, how we will share this information. What words can we use that will be direct and helpful, but not accusatory or shaming?

It's so important, although sometimes hard, to remember that we'll all make mistakes as we muddle through this, and at one point or another we'll all likely be the parents of a victim, a bully, a joiner-inner, and a bystander. The goal is to support each other.

I asked some of my friends what words they'd take as helpful, and here's what they came up with:

Here's what I saw, I thought you'd want to know.

Have you seen this?

FYI.

The common thread among everyone I asked is that every parent wanted to know what was going on with his or her kids.

When I first started looking at Instagram with mom-eyes versus user-eyes, it was like putting on a pair of glasses or contacts without knowing I'd actually needed them. People who get glasses or contacts for the first time often describe how clear, vivid, and detailed the world becomes. The world around them—outlines of clouds, blades of grass, leaves in trees—all becomes suddenly, shockingly visible. This is how I felt about looking at Instagram as a mom about to let her tween use the platform.

I realized that who our kids follow is just as important to know as who's following them. Here's what I saw and what I learned.

Example: Instagram "Home"

When I use Instagram, I mostly stay in my feed, designated by the "home" icon, where I see what the people I follow are posting.

Example: Instagram "You"

KINDNESS WINS

I also browse in my "You" tab, where I see the interactions people I follow have with the photos I post. I use Twitter in the exact same way.

Example: Instagram "Following"

But there's a whole other tab, "Following," where you can see the interactions the people you're following are having with all the people *they're* following.

This suddenly opens up your feed to a whole slew of information and experiences that you might have never signed up for.

When I looked at my kids' friends' profiles, even if they were set to private, I could see how many people follow them and how many people they follow. One nice, sweet girl I'd known for years had approximately 300 followers and was following over 1,000 people!

This jarred me enough to drop her mom a simple note: *I saw your sweet girl's account on Instagram. She's following over 1,000 people, which means she can see what they all post and what they all like and comment on. I thought you'd want to know. Let me know if you want to talk about it. Ugh, so much to learn with these loves of ours!*

And I left it at that. I'll be honest with you and admit that my heart skipped a teeny-tiny beat before I sent that e-mail. I would never want to put anyone on the defensive. But I sent it anyway because my own insecurities were far less important than someone else's online safety.

Her mom wrote back almost instantly, and we went out for a cup of coffee so I could show her what I just showed you. A week or so later, the four of us—moms and girls—got together to discuss the exact same things.

My friend and her daughter had an important conversation, and they're both looking at who she's following a little bit more critically now.

The boy whose pictures are suddenly not being "liked," the girl who's commenting on photos during the school day, the boy who's getting into an argument on someone else's photo comment thread or commenting on a stranger's thread—these are all puzzle pieces of information that are helpful to know as a parent. So share with others what you would want someone to share with you.

3 Takeaways:

- Scrolling when you see online bullying is the equivalent of walking away when you see it in person.
- Saying "Stop" to a bully is hard. Saying "Stop" to a friend is harder. Kids need defusing words that are easy for them to say and to type.
- Teach your kids to tell you when they see troublesome online behavior. If they can identify cyberbullying, they can be a part of stopping it.

58

Chapter 4

A Picture Is Worth a Thousand (Nice) Words

"All I can do is follow my instincts, because I'll never please everyone."
— Emma Watson

I spent what used to feel like forever—but what now seems like an eyelash blink—with a preschooler by my side, a toddler in my lap, and an infant in a car seat crossing his chubby little fingers that he might get a smidge of undivided attention.

Jason and I don't live near family and his work hours are long, which means that back then, my work days were bleary.

I was bone-tired. My shoulders ached from meeting my kids' needs during the day and my eyes were half-lidded from meeting their needs at night. We ran errands slowly, not very efficiently, and with all four of us present at every single appointment.

Doctor's visits were especially painful. For reasons I truly can't explain, I used to schedule everyone's wellness checks for the same day, forgetting in the months between visits that the pain of getting out the door and into the doctor's office was nothing compared to the long "being good" time required when you choose to have back-to-back appointments for three kids under the age of five.

At the end of one of these marathon appointments, our pediatrician slipped out to get forms or pamphlets or medicine, and I slipped over. Over the edge, that is.

It was a teeny-tiny windowless office with sleek white floors bookended by beige walls. Facing me was a single poster. It portrayed a mama with a sparkling smile and sleek hair holding a giggling baby, his lips parted in a gummy grin, a wisp of hair atop his head.

The real-life scene beneath the poster was anything but picture perfect. Under the unforgiving (at best) fluorescent lights, there was twirling and crying and whining and so, so very much talking. Someone needed a diaper change, someone else was unloading the diaper bag. That pristine office was polka dotted with swirls of our mess and our noise, and in that instant I was done.

As I was whispering not-so-sweet nothings at my children, the doctor stepped back into the room. I don't know if she heard my words or just recognized my tears forming, my cheeks burning, and my shoulders slumping, but she saw what was going on. I was sitting on the floor surrounded by the contents of our bag, helping with a shoe, zipping a jacket, and rocking a car seat, when she looked down and said, "Wow, you're all doing a good job."

She didn't elaborate or give advice or offer to help, although any of these would have been appropriate. She just saw a snapshot—I was struggling—and decided to comment on the good that she saw instead of the bad.

We can apply this same "search for the goodness" rule to commenting on photos that we see online.

What we know about photos is that, much like hard parenting moments, people love commenting on them. Instagram is an entire platform based on people's love, passion, and sometimes obsession with the interplay of photos and comments.

Photos are slices of people's lives that they deem important and share-worthy. But once people share their photos, they're as vulnerable as I was as a new-ish mom having a bad day in the pediatrician's office. And what photos—and people—deserve is the same type of kindness that our doctor showed me.

Sometimes commenting takes a turn for the worse and is overtly mean via insults. These comments are simple to pinpoint, discuss, and fix. But sometimes the meanness is covert and harder to spot. An example of this is when comments or "likes" are used as a social currency, given to boost or withheld to "lower."

So what do we do about that?

It would work to go through your own feed and create mock comments with your child. Do you have to click "like" and add comments to every thread you scroll past? Absolutely not. In fact you shouldn't, because there are friends, sports, books, parents, and siblings to connect with offline.

We have to use our own judgment here and make repeated good choices and teach our kids to do the same. The main question to constantly ask is *why* are you choosing to "like" or not to "like," to comment or not to comment?

The reason withholding is such a powerful bullying tool is that if you're constantly online, everyone can see whose photos you've "liked" or commented on. So when they see that you've "liked" one hundred photos but not theirs, it makes them feel bad. Right or wrong, this is how it is.

Do you remember being young and worrying about what others thought of you or how much people liked you or how many people liked you? Do you remember, like I do, slipping into these same angsty thoughts yesterday or the day before that? "Like" currency on social media is like that. But it feels suffocatingly loud because you can see and compare—tangibly—how many "likes" you have with how many everyone else has.

It's important to teach and to model to our kids how to transcend this. Of course it is. But it's also important to acknowledge that the jealousy and insecurity that's bred within "like" currency is real. And that their role in it is, too.

So the only solution to this is to limit how much time we spend on social media and to ensure that we're being kind whenever we are online. When I'm online, I click-click-click all the "likes" I can, and I comment kindly on all the photos I see. But I never try to catch up on what's posted while I'm offline.

We can teach our kids this time limit and we can talk about how "like" currency works and how they want to use it.

We can teach our kids that commenting online is the exact same thing as saying something directly to someone's face.

We can teach our kids to get into the habits of slowing down and taking notice if there's someone who may need a little kindness. Then we can teach them to drop love bombs with wild abandon. Not many "likes" on that girl's picture? *Click.* That boy's picture doesn't have any comments? *Be the first one.* It doesn't hurt to be kind. Not ever. So we can teach our kids to be recklessly kind online—for a limited time each day.

And most importantly, we can teach our kids that they're in charge of their online lives and that they can—and should—walk away any time their gut tells them it's the right thing to do. This lesson is as simple as asking them if they've ever gotten that feeling in their bellies or hearts or minds that something isn't quite right, and perhaps sharing a time when you've had this happen. Tell them that paying attention to that feeling is the absolute right thing to do. Whether it's standing up against unkind behavior or just being ready to log off for the night, it's important to teach our kids that their instincts are valuable and should be heeded.

1 Resource:

"Parenting as a Gen Xer: We're the First Generation of Parents in the Age of iEverything" by Allison Slater Tate on *WashingtonPost.com* is a thoughtfully reflective essay about the new terrain of parenting that you and I are exploring as we're straddling the line of having kids who've never known a world without the Internet at their fingertips, while we were raised without it.

2 Things to Talk About:

Discuss with Your Kids

Sit down with your kids and talk about being mindful of the amount of time they spend on Facebook or Instagram or whatever platform they'd like to start with. I definitely recommend practicing with one platform at a time. Scroll through your feed, their feed, or their friends' feeds and have them point out what they'd "like," what they'd comment on and how, when they'd keep scrolling, and when they'd sign off. Remind them to consider other people's photos as opportunities to compliment, "like," or scroll, and that's all. Ever.

I did this with my kids before they had social media accounts of their own. When our kids reach a certain age, the amount of value they give our opinions teeters lower, while the value they give their peers' opinions edges higher. Why not open the conversation while we're still on the high end of things?

We should also discuss with our kids the kinds of photos they may post. Get them used to looking at posts from different points of view. Talk to them about uncomfortable things like how an older boy might see their photo, or a younger girl, or their grandma. Talk about body shots, unflattering photos of their friends, and photos that clearly show where they are, where they go to school, and who's with them.

Each of these needs to be a short, repeated conversation.

One way I model smart social media behavior for my daughter is by posting a photo or a status after I leave a place rather than as soon as I get there, and we discuss the safety reasons behind why I do this. When she looks over my shoulder while I'm Instagramming, I let her see the (kind) comments I write on the photos I see, and we talk about what I'm doing in these cases as well. One of my daughter's friends consistently seems to "like" everyone's photos on Instagram. I love pointing out and discussing the kindness in her actions, too.

I don't bring up examples every single time I encounter them, but I do consider these teachable moments, and I grasp at them consciously and regularly.

One tricky topic to cover is posting and tagging photos with friends. We need to help our kids dissect how not being in a photo might make someone else feel. If a friend was invited to an outing but couldn't make it, it would be a-okay to post when considering the situation from her point of view. But if someone wasn't invited and might be hurt by that, maybe that outing doesn't need to be shared. Not everything does.

You'll need to maneuver this fuzzy terrain together. There isn't a "blanket rule" for this one, just a nudge to make sure that you're posting for the right reasons. Making someone feel left out isn't one.

Discuss with Your Peers

What will you do if someone you care about and are connected to crosses the kindness line? Will you send her a private message saying that what she posted might hurt your mutual friend's feelings? Will you respond to her hurtful comment in an open thread? Every situation and how we each handle it may look different, and that's okay. What's important is getting into the habit of expecting kindness and being surprised by bullying, and not the other way around.

You might be asking yourself if a situation like this is worth starting a kerfuffle over. I say yes. Why shouldn't you be the one to do the right thing? If not you, then who?

On my Facebook page I love posing questions that I think many of us have on our minds. *How old should kids be to have a phone? What will you tell your kids about your experiences with alcohol? What is new math?* But when I post a question, I make myself available to respond to all commenters with kindness and respect—the ones who agree with me and the ones who don't. I've very rarely had people be rude to each other in a thread, but I always step in when it happens. Always.

One summer day, my kids were playing in the backyard. It was a golden morning. The sun hit the windows in slices as their voices rose and fell, mirroring their bodies as they pumped their legs, willing their swings higher and higher. My kids were young, not quite school-aged, and I was watching them from our patio table. A man with two young children crossed into our backyard and asked my kids if his children could play on our swing set. I later learned that he was a neighbor's son visiting for the weekend, but we'd never met, so to my kids and me he was a stranger.

I wasn't visible from where he was, and he hadn't made contact with me with his eyes or his words, so as far as I could tell the only permission he asked for was theirs. At the time, I hadn't experienced anything like this, and I was caught off guard. "Sure," is what my kids said; "ohmygod," is what I thought. Jason and I had talked to the kids about not getting into cars with strangers, but letting strangers into our backyard was apparently fair game.

In that moment, my kids played hostesses and host, and I went over to the man and introduced myself. But that evening, our family discussed what I thought should've happened, which is that their answer should've been something along the lines of, "We have to ask our mom," and then they should've walked all the way up the hill together to actually ask me.

All in all, this was a teachable moment for our family. Everyone has different boundaries and expectations of how to handle situations like these. I couldn't help but wonder if I was spot on with my discomfort in the moment or if I was overreacting. So later that night, I did what we do in our social-media-infused lives, and I took the question to

Facebook, calling on my virtual village to discuss what they thought about this experience.

The opinions were strong, albeit respectful. Many of my friends thought that crossing yards, and play sets, was lovely and community-building. Some thought that my neighbor's son should have rang our doorbell to make sure I was home. And still others thought he should have encouraged my kids to ask me for permission.

I stayed in the conversation as long as I could, and when I left it, it was for the night. When I came back in the morning, I saw that two of my friends had gotten into a debate about the topic. They were writing with perspective and language and life experience between them and they were misunderstanding each other's points of view. While neither one had said anything mean to the other, they were both clearly on the defensive.

In this case, I decided to message each of them privately and share what I knew about the other that I thought might help defuse their hurt feelings and bring them closer to understanding each other.

I didn't need to say much more than a sentence or two. They both reentered the conversation with kinder, more open words.

I know that this was my situation to handle because it happened on my Facebook page. But what if we all treated interactions like these as our own? Someone once told me, "If you see it, it's yours." I think this applies here. If we see someone hurting, someone being unkind, someone needing kindness, then all of the above become our chances, our moments, our opportunities to help.

If we all maneuvered online in this way, I think that misunderstandings would fizzle out more often and more quickly. I also think that people who are rude, mean, or out of line on purpose would lose their reign.

3 Takeaways:

- You're in charge of your online life.
- You have "like" currency. Use it kindly.
- If you see it, it's yours.

Chapter 5
We Don't Talk about Other People's Bodies

"I mean, if we're regulating cigarettes and sex and cuss words because of the effect they have on our younger generation, why aren't we regulating things like calling people fat?"
— Jennifer Lawrence

When Jason and I joined our gym, we were given a tour of the entire facility from the pool to the weight room to the group fitness studio. I stood outside of that last room on the top floor, bookended by Jason and the gym manager, listening to the music pulsing behind the double doors and seeing the people on the other side of them moving in unison.

I wondered why the manager decided to not only bring us here but to also pause to peer inside those doors. *Do I look like someone who would ever go in there?* I thought. Years (and years) of being a girl with body and food issues had taught me one thing: fitness wasn't friendly.

Fast-forward to today and that studio is my second home. I have a regular spot that I veer toward in every class. To my credit, I only twitch slightly when someone else takes it. My gym friends checked on me when our family dog died, my Zumba teacher gave me a coupon for cute workout pants she thought I'd like, and the lady at the front desk pronounces my name correctly. I'm a regular.

Once I realized that I am, in fact, "someone who would go in there," it was liberating and exciting. I tried a variety of classes and was riding the high of the nice people (endorphins!) and the loud music (to move in unison to!).

One week, by the time I got to Zumba, there was already someone in my regular spot. I shook it off and stood next to someone new. *Meeting new friends! That's a benefit of going to the gym*, I thought. So I introduced myself. She was decked out in designer workout wear, from her Athleta headband to her Lululemon pants. She wore her hair short and tucked behind her ears. Her laugh lines were pronounced. I liked her instantly. She quickly assessed that I was new-ish and before we traded stories, or even names, she said, "You'll lose that weight with this class!"

I hadn't said anything about wanting to lose weight. I spoke about loving the class, the teacher, the music. When I felt her eyes run up and down my body, I was uncomfortable at best and humiliated on contact.

My new friend—I consider her one today—didn't mean any harm with her words. She thought she was helping me, motivating me perhaps, by being a regular gym-goer passing along knowledge to a newbie. But that's not what I heard when she spoke. What she was offering in motivation, I scooped up as shame.

In my experience, girls' bodies are assessed and talked about much too often. You're so thin/fat/hot/not. And although I'm not a boy, I've been told that the pressure is equally acute for them. Oh my goodness, enough. We all need to (please) agree that other people's bodies aren't up for discussion.

GALIT BREEN

When Jason and I got the e-mail asking if we'd like to film an interview for *Inside Edition* about the article I'd just published, *I Wrote an Article about Marriage, and All Anyone Noticed Is That I'm Fat*, we were watching the *Today* show segment about the same article.

Several days earlier, a producer from the *Today* show had tweeted me to get permission to tell my story (and to check how to pronounce my name!). When I first saw the tweet, I thought it was spam—why would the *Today* show want to discuss me? So when Jason read the *Inside Edition* producer's e-mail over my shoulder, he jokingly asked, "Is this spam, too?"

Much to my surprise, neither the e-mail nor the tweet were a joke or spam, and less than three hours later, we were recording our *Inside Edition* segment. When we got to the studio, a producer sat us down, handed us earbuds and microphones, and got started right away. No prep, no thinking time, not even a chance to brush our hair. During our drive over, we'd lightly discussed what we might be asked. But we assumed that we'd get a preview of the questions before we started recording.

We were wrong about that. We were also wrong in our predictions that the interviewer would start the conversation on a lighter note and dig into the nitty-gritty details as we warmed up. The second question she asked each of us was, "What's your message to America?" To say that at first blush we were unprepared to answer this question is an understatement. But one heartbeat later, it felt simple and natural and obvious to say, "We don't talk about other people's bodies."

This is non-negotiable.

We never know what someone is dealing with or what we might trigger. What we see as a compliment or advice or just helping, might not be taken or heard in the same way. The reason so many people took interest in my experience with cyberbullying was because they could relate. And while we can't control how other people feel, we can control what comes out of our own mouths.

It's been said that the words people say to us and about us become our own self-talk. I've found this to be true. For days, perhaps weeks, I heard the negative comments I'd received on this article whispering in my ear, typing in my mind. I've found this self-talk to be damaging in the moment and extremely hard to undo in the long term.

This is why we need to stay away from commenting on and labeling other people's bodies, both in person and online.

1 Resource:

"I Wrote an Article about Marriage, and All Anyone Noticed Is That I'm Fat" is the article I wrote on *xoJane.com* about how it feels when people talk about our bodies, and how I felt when online commenters discussed my weight in an unrelated thread. The consequences of body talk ripple widely. We can all do better than misusing that power.

2 Things to Talk About:

Discuss with Your Kids

Sit down with your kids and talk about body image and how commenting on someone else's body is never okay. There's nothing shameful about bodies at all. But you're only in charge of your own body. So many issues would be solved if we all understood this.

If you say, see, or hear things like, "She has a great body," "He's fat," or even, "Have you lost weight?" step in

GALIT BREEN

and have the conversation, "We don't talk about other people's bodies."

In my *xoJane.com* article, I screencapped and shared three of the comments that people had left on my article about marriage.

WE GET IT! Huffnpuff..you love fat women..we get it... enough is enough.........

I LOVE LOVE LOVE that you used a picture of a bigger girl as the bride! Bravo Huffington Post!!!!

One thing you didn't learn is "don't marry a heifer."

I didn't delete names or sugarcoat words—I wanted to stun people. And I did. Friends and strangers alike shared my article with empowering messages that body talk is unacceptable.

But not too long after my article and message went viral, I noted several of my friends—some of the same smart, savvy feminists who had just shared my article and introduced it with their own call for action to end body talk —posting photos of shirtless guys and calling them hot, sexy, welcome, and wanted.

I know that not a single one of these women were doing anything purposefully wrong. They were being playful and fun. But they were missing an important piece of this discussion. Commenting on both women's and men's bodies is equally inappropriate. There are very few times it's okay to discuss someone else's body in either hurtful or complimentary ways.

We can have these conversations with our kids and teach them to balk at, rather then expect, body talk.

Discuss with Your Peers

This is a tricky one to discuss with peers, because even though we, as adults, have been told to not insult others' bodies, many people still think that complimenting bodies and giving helpful weight loss advice is okay.

It's not.

Speak up. "I actually don't think we should comment on other people's bodies," is hard to say, but try it. Explain why.

When my wedding photos ended up on *Upworthy.com*, the commenters there tried, not unkindly, to console me by saying, "But she's not even fat!" Believe it or not, this didn't make me feel better.

I still felt like I was being examined by other people's searingly scrutinizing eyes and that I was at the mercy of their quick-typing fingertips, waiting for their approval. And whether or not I was actually fat in the photos missed the point. If I was, would it have been okay for people to make those kinds of comments? Spoiler alert: No. No, it wouldn't have been. My body isn't here to be assessed by other people. No one else's is either.

When you're trying to (kindly) help someone else understand this, try this line of reasoning: If someone asks for your opinion and help, and you're a dietician, a fitness expert, a physician, or a trainer, give it. But if no one asks and you're not trained to help, move on. Not your circus, not your monkeys.

3 Takeaways:

- We don't talk about other people's bodies.
- We don't talk about other people's bodies.
- We don't talk about other people's bodies.

Chapter 6

If You Wouldn't Say It or Show It to Your Mama, Keep It Offline

"I've never been shy or secretive with the fact that if you walk into my life, you may be walking onto a record."
— Taylor Swift

I was at an event at my kids' school. A mother I knew on a surface level but wasn't connected to in the usual ways—our kids weren't the same age, our husbands didn't know each other, we weren't Facebook friends—started engaging my kids in small talk.

It was a tight space with lots of people crisscrossing our path, so I was only able to half-hear their conversation. "What's your favorite song?" I caught her asking my daughter, who was a young and precocious preschooler at the time.

I looked around, waved at a teacher, wondered where Jason was, and I focused back in. "Do you like any *other* songs?" She was still asking my daughter about her musical interests.

When I tuned more fully into the conversation, I could see how lighthearted and earnest this woman was being.

KINDNESS WINS

There was a smile playing on her lips, and her eyes were sparkling.

And then it clicked for me. She was trying to get my daughter to tell her something she already knew. I'd recently written an article about my kids walking into their preschool singing the song "Fat Bottomed Girls." I loved the show *Glee* at the time and the song was on one of the series CDs that we listened to on an endless loop in the car.

The incident had been more fun and anecdote-worthy than embarrassing, so I wrote about it and this woman had read it.

Because we didn't know each other very well and I'd never told her the story, I assumed she didn't know about it. That was my mistake. Because the thing about posting online is that you just don't know who's going to see—or share—your posts. And that's how you have to act—as if everyone is looking.

One of my girls leans toward privacy. What I tell her over and over again is to expect very little privacy online both with her peers and with her dad and me. Anyone can see what you post. Anyone.

Privacy is a topic that needs to be discussed and re-discussed over and over (and over) again. Short, repeated lessons come into play here for a purposeful reason. When we feel close and connected to our friends, we tend to forget what we know about boundaries. Almost always, this works to our benefit and allows us to form closer relationships and friendships. For tweens and teens who crave both, this is important and shouldn't be discouraged or stopped. But when our guard is down, our borders loosen and our vulnerability heightens. This is where mistakes happen for both adults and kids.

We often wonder why kids do things that seem so obviously not in their best interests, like taking and sending body photos or bad-mouthing friends or teachers in e-mails or texts that are so easily sharable. This is why. They want to connect and, in that wanting, they forget the ground rules.

As our kids spend time on social media, gain confidence about their online presence, and begin to truly enjoy their online interactions with their friends, they may forget the lessons we've taught them. The conversations we had the day we gave them their phones and Instagram accounts will be muted, and what will be more important to them is their friends and the desire to be close to them.

So we need to become that consistent presence over their shoulders until their internal voice takes over with the same messages.

When Jason and I gave our daughter her phone, she was most excited to text with a close friend. They immediately began texting emojis and jokes and *What are you doings?* One day, my daughter's friend asked if she wanted to FaceTime. She did, of course, and I gave her the go-ahead.

Kids have a ridiculous amount of chatting and messaging apps available to them, from ooVoo—which allows group chats—to Kik—a texting app with a wealth of sharing abilities that relies on user names rather than phone numbers, making it a cross between a social media site and a private-use app. The fun and the connectivity that apps like these provide are wonderful. The opportunities for oversharing that they offer, however, are not.

Some parents choose to adjust the app rating restrictions on their kids' devices to prevent the download of apps they'd rather their kids not use. But this doesn't replace the conversations we need to have with our kids about how to use apps like these or even more private ones like FaceTime. I learned that from my daughter's first FaceTime experience.

Moments after she asked if she could FaceTime with her friend, the girls were facing each other via their devices. Right after, "Hi," what I heard was, "Who's home?" My daughter's sweet friend was home alone and was curious if she was, too, and my daughter answered her truthfully—I was home but would be leaving soon to run errands.

Jason and I had talked to the kids ad nauseam about not announcing when they're home alone. "Don't answer the door," we said. "Ignore the phone," we added. Our kids knew this perfectly. But in that moment, excited to talk to her friend, to connect and to be connected, she forgot. In this case, my daughter was just fine to share who was home and who wasn't, because I was home with her, but this was a great reminder to discuss when we'd prefer her to not share this information and why.

When my daughter got off the phone that day, it was the perfect time to revisit privacy, what needs to be shared and when, and what we share when we're home alone.

In this situation, we practiced the actual words she'd say if she was already, or about to be, home alone. Without the words on the tip of her tongue, the truth rolls out awfully easily. What a strange exercise it is to help your child practice telling a lie! I explained to her that my purpose in this lie-coaching was that I wanted her to send the message that there's at least one adult at home. I want this to be a habit before she's a teen and "home alone" carries with it a whole slew of possibilities besides FaceTiming jokes and silly faces. At the time, we were on the cusp of discussing what these home-alone possibilities included, and I considered this our conversation opener.

The word "private" is also used to describe account statuses, and this is a guise that makes our kids feel even safer and more confident to forget what we've taught them. You, like me, might hear things along the lines of, "See, Mom? Only the people we approve to follow me can ever see my posts." Wrong. Nope. Not true.

Setting our kids' account statuses to "private" allows for a certain peace of mind—we don't have to worry about strangers having access to their photos. But what we know about bullying is that it's not always—or even often—strangers whom we need to worry about. When we were young, our bullies weren't usually strangers. They were the kids who passed mean notes about us in class, the ones who didn't let us sit at their table during lunch, and the ones who tripped us in the hallway or embarrassed us in gym class. We knew them and, in some cases, so did our parents.

In the case of strangers versus someone we know, cyberbullying isn't all that different from the playground bullying of our youth and nightmares. Cyberbullying awareness advocate Sue Scheff explains that according to a Cox Communications Survey, 81 percent of young people think bullying online is easier to get away with than bullying in person. Scheff then goes on to cite a shudder-worthy statistic: approximately four out of ten kids (42 percent) have experienced cyberbullying.

I would bet that a very small number, if any, of these bullies were strangers to the kids they were bullying. So when it comes to cyberbullying, a "private" account may not do the trick; it may not protect our kids.

There's another reason that privacy settings can provide a false sense of security. A photo shared on an Instagram account that's set to private and has approximately one hundred approved followers is initially only visible to those followers. But any one of those approved "friends"—who on any given day may be hormonal, moody, or impulsive—can very simply capture, save, and share this photo with their followers.

I, for example, could capture and share a photo like this with my 6,000 Twitter followers or 1,500 Facebook friends. And guess what? Each of those people could then share this (private!) photo with his or her networks, growing this number exponentially to way more than the original one hundred or so approved followers.

It really is that easy for this to happen. And the same is true for the words you type in comments and shares.

If you don't want that photo or comment to be seen by everyone you know, then you shouldn't put it online.

You'll find directions for a screencapping and sharing exercise listed in the References section at the end of this book. Take a look at it and then literally show your child how easy it is to take a photo from private to not so much.

Now use this lack of privacy to your advantage.

When my daughter asked my husband and me about getting an Instagram account, what I told her was this: "You have to be so open with us about what you're posting and what your friends are posting and why. So when we sit together and you clam up about a topic because you're uncomfortable or embarrassed or you want privacy, then I know you're not ready."

Open the lines of communication in this way. Our kids will talk because they want those accounts. Is that sneaky? Maybe. But it's also an excellent lesson that there isn't anything private—at all—about what you post online.

Tell your kids to really think about that before they post. Do they want you, their grandma, their teachers, the cute boy from down the street, or the mean girl next door to see that post? If not, then they shouldn't post it.

Some platforms, like Facebook, allow you to segment who you show what to via lists and settings. You can use technology to your benefit in this way. But remember that once it's out there it can be screencapped and shared. This is why body shots, for example, are never (truly, never) a good idea.

1 Resource:

"A Letter to My Daughters about Weed" by Dan Shapiro on *OpenSalon.com* is a lightly written and incredibly transparent post about marijuana, told in the form of a letter from the author to his daughters. My favorite line in this piece is this: *Why I, or any other parent, would leave you on your own to think this through is beyond me.* We have to help our kids maneuver through the tough things. It's our job. And when we are transparent with them, it gives them the freedom to be transparent with us.

2 Things to Talk About:

Discuss with Your Kids

Sit down with your kids and literally show them how easy it is to share their online choices with others—friends and strangers alike. Liberally repeat the phrase, "You should have very, very low privacy expectations."

By the way, many people view this lack of privacy as one of the detriments of using social media. And when it's misused, this is, indeed, true. But when you use social media kindly and ethically and with the full knowledge of how visibly transparent your sharing is, this is actually freeing and an excellent reminder that your online self should mirror-image your real-life self.

Use this lens to discuss what's good sharing fodder, what's not, and why.

Practice this a million-bajillion times. For example, why do we not share pictures of our bodies or body parts? So many reasons. Discuss them.

And when it comes to the comments your kids type … Have them read their own words out loud, say them using a different tone, and imagine saying the same comment to you, or the person they commented at saying it to their parents. If none of the above makes them cringe, then they're good to go. If any of it gives them pause, then it's time to edit or delete.

Discuss with Your Peers

You might be thinking that what your peers post online is none of your business. And, to some extent, you're absolutely right. I'm all for everyone taking a few small steps away from telling each other what to do.

But sometimes it is our business and that sometimes is when other people's actions affect our kids or our family.

Mull over how you feel about friends posting photos of your kids. What about tagging them at events? Sharing their words or photos?

My rule of thumb for posting is to always ask before sharing a photo of anyone—this includes my kids and my husband. And if anyone says, "*No, thank you*," I respect that.

As for friends sharing and tagging my kids or me in photos and check-ins or sharing things like screen caps of our text messages, I find this arena to be as fuzzy as talking to our kids about sharing photos with their friends. I don't have a blanket rule for this.

If the share really bothers my kids or me or it somehow crosses any of our privacy lines, then I (respectfully) ask my friend to remove it. If it irks me, but is let-go-able, then I do that.

Remember that everyone feels differently when it comes to this. Be mindful and respectful of others' boundaries and a non-apologetic advocate of your own.

3 Takeaways:

- Nothing is private online.
- Everything is sharable.
- "You need to be open with me if you want to be online."

Chapter 7

Learn How to Discuss Hard Things

"I don't like a tremendous amount of conflict. I don't think that fighting and passion are the same thing."
— Tina Fey

In our first year of marriage, every disagreement Jason and I had was a fight. As in a full-blown, drawn-out, negotiation-and-making-up-requiring fight.

Toilet paper facing the "wrong" way? Fight.

New brand of cereal? Fight.

Towels folded differently, Thanksgiving with your family and not mine, spent an extra $50 at the grocery store? Fight, fight, and one more fight.

Having kids gave us a whole new slew of topics to fight about. Like everyone in this world, we were raised differently and approached each new parenting experience with our own baggage and assumptions about how things should be.

This was true from the very beginning.

When I was pregnant with our oldest, Jason and I planned every detail of our upcoming hospital stay. We filled our bags, packed our clothes, and called our people. I wanted to invite everyone we knew to welcome her into the world, and Jason wanted some privacy—family only. (It turns out that he was absolutely right. Don't tell him.)

We had that fight sitting on our yellow couch, the first big purchase we ever made together. We started off looking into each other's eyes, but by the end of the "conversation," we were probably glaring.

We both knew with every fiber of our (righteous) beings that the other person was wrong. And more than that, we knew that the other person was wronging us.

Through our years together we've learned so much. How to let things go, how to compromise, how to fight issues instead of each other, and how to admit that we don't always know what to do or what the answers are.

Within these lessons, we had to learn how to disagree. Marriage is filled with daily decisions, from the minutiae of menus and car pools to the heart-splaying ones circling around belief systems. The most important agreement we ever made is that we're on the same team and we need to act like it, even if we disagree about the topic we're discussing.

I was taught to never discuss religion or politics (or which way the toilet paper goes!) in public company because these topics can be hard and awkward and people get so riled discussing them. I've found this to be true. But it's not where the problem with fighting lies.

The issue is that we've lost—or never found—the art of disagreeing with each other.

So instead of engaging in dialogue that can potentially better us both, instead of pausing to listen and learn, we either rage against the other person, mute them, or make instant decisions about how wrong they are. Change can't be made, knowledge can't be exchanged, and closeness can't be gained from any one of these behaviors.

What if it didn't have to be this way? We could make it our goal to figure out how to engage in dialogue and how to approach each other in order to understand instead of to convince. The key lies in intentionally shifting our reason for entering a conversation to actually hearing what someone else has to say even though—because?—that person's opinion differs from ours.

And if we find ourselves engaged in a conversation that's out of our comfort zone, a beautiful response is simply saying, "I don't know." It's akin to, "I'm listening." We aren't required to have solid experiences with and opinions about every topic of conversation that arises. It's just as—if not more—valuable to be present by listening.

The beauty of the Internet is that, much like our yellow couch, it brings people together. It's as if people, with their different experiences and hearts and thoughts and opinions, are all in one place with the chance to learn from each other (literally) at their fingertips.

This can be seen as a chance to convince others of our points of view. But what if, instead, we flipped this narrative and chose to see it as an opportunity to find out what others know and really think?

Admitting we don't know is a great first step. When we do this, we're opening the door to conversations and to each other. We can let go of the responsibility of convincing others to think like we do. All we really need to do is engage in dialogue. The good news is that this is a much simpler, and more enjoyable, goal to attain.

I've learned that more often than not, the most heated conversations happen because both sides—both opinions, both people—are right in one way or another. This is possible and true and surmountable and can lead to great conversations about difficult topics.

KINDNESS WINS

When we started dating, Jason and I were in a long-distance relationship. We met online when it was still gasp-worthy and new to do so. I was living in California, a first-year teacher by day and a graduate student by night, and Jason was living in Wisconsin working toward his degree in music education. Because we were both on a school schedule, where there are many planned breaks and days off for holidays and vacations, we were able to spend practically one week out of every month together. I'd visit his college town and fumble my way through his music classes, and he'd slip into my teaching and learning schedule, reading while I studied and charming my students while I taught.

This unusual schedule of ours also meant that we joined each other's families for holidays earlier in our relationship than might have been expected. When Jason arrived at his parents' house for Thanksgiving that year, I was by his side. We immediately began filling our weekend with the dates we couldn't have throughout the month. An afternoon movie, a Tae Soo Do class at his studio, dinner with his friends.

By the second day his family was visibly, and rightfully, irked with us. This wasn't just our weekend together, it was also one of the few weekends that his whole family was able to be together under one roof. Jason and I hadn't yet learned the art of balancing our time, and while we were right to want to spend the weekend dating, his family was right in wanting to carve out time together as well.

Today, as a parent, I understand the value of family time spent sans the spaces created by schedules and work and distance. This knowledge tugs at every single one of my heartstrings. But at the same time, I remember all too well the overwhelming sadness that was a side effect of our monthly good-byes and the long-distance nature of our relationship. So I also know that, on that Thanksgiving weekend, all of our feelings were justified. All of our perspectives were right.

This is why all of our emotions were heightened and all of our feelings were hurt. And it's also why when Jason's family became vocal about their disappointment in how the weekend was going, Jason and I were tempted to cocoon ourselves and ignore what we were being told by the storytellers facing us.

More often than not, this is the case when people disagree. So instead of proving our rightness and someone else's wrongness, what we really need to do is learn how to kindly—with thoughts based in our own truths—disagree. We need to agree to see things differently without taking the conversation personally or using it as an excuse to attack someone else, ignore them, or barrage them with our opinions. I tell my kids that if they're only hearing their own voices speaking for a while, then it's time to let someone else speak. The same can be said about online dialogue. Share the floor—or the Facebook thread—with others.

We need to engage in dialogue and share our experiences, we need to listen when others share theirs, and we need to avoid name-calling, disrespecting, or dismissing others.

Online disagreements can get just as muddy and murky as family weekends can. One of my friends scrolls through her son's Instagram feed weekly. One evening, when she looked at his account, she saw that he'd recently commented on a picture of a rainbow flag. So she clicked the photo to see for herself what was said. Our state was amidst the debate about marriage equality at the time, and his words were ones of support. But when someone else, a stranger commenting on the same photo, chimed in with negative, cruel words, my friend's son engaged him and met his negativity with his own. He called this commenter out for the bully he was being, which his mom thought was good. But he also name-called and used some abusive words of his own. My friend took away his phone for that.

When he was gifted his phone and his account, his parents had told him this would happen if he used unsavory language online, so he wasn't surprised by this. But I was. "But he did the right thing!" I questioned. "But in the wrong way," she answered. And she was right.

Discussion and dialogue are good game-changers. Salty language, no matter how justified we feel it is, just isn't.

We can have real discussions without name-calling or ignoring. I bet our online and real-life interactions and relationships will be better for it when we do.

1 Resource:

"Rude Reactions, Angry Outbursts, and Ladders That Lift" by Rachel Macy Stafford on *HandsFreeMama.com* is a personal essay told in Stafford's kind, wise voice giving the reader a gentle reminder that in debates and disagreements and heated moments, we shouldn't make the other person's perspective about us. When we avoid doing this, we're able to approach topics—and people—in a non-fighting stance. This makes dialogue and kindness possible.

2 Things to Talk About:

Discuss with Your Kids

Sit down with your kids and discuss what to do and say when they disagree with someone online. This direct conversation is key.

But this is also one of the many things we're going to have to teach by example.

Debate with your kids, engage in conversations with them, disagree with them, and allow them to disagree with you. Model learning, listening, and choosing words based in truth and kindness. Point out when either one of you does this right.

And when you do it wrong? Apologize! This is a golden, maybe even a platinum, lesson. If kindness wins, accountability rules. We need to show our kids how to come back from a mistake with grace by owning it, apologizing for it, and moving forward.

And, on the flipside, we need to model what to do if someone offends us and then owns it by apologizing, mending, and attempting to move forward. We need to show them—whether they're strangers, friends, or our children—the same grace we'd want shown to us. We have to let them back in and move forward together.

One of my girls went through a forgetful stage, which meant that on any given day she couldn't find her homework, her lunchbox, her winter gloves, or on one notable below-zero-degree day, her winter coat. The truth is that she's still in this "phase" and may always be. The other truth is this trait grates on me because I have it, too.

So when our family is frantic and harried and late and I see the look in her eyes that I now recognize as meaning she's lost something yet again, sometimes I handle it well and sometimes I just don't.

One morning, as we were trying to get out the door for school, I had a "just don't handle it well" moment.

She insisted that she'd left her gloves on the kitchen table the night before, and that in the morning they'd (magically) disappeared. I was more than dubious. This wasn't my first rodeo, and my accumulated frustration and assumptions from every time she'd ever lost something—or we ran late because we couldn't find whatever it was she was missing—came into my mind and out of my mouth. I was frustrated, and she was hurt.

But when we all peeled off our winter layers and helped her look, we found what she was looking for—I'd put other misplaced things on top of her gloves. They were where she'd left them. Covered, but still there. She was right and I was wrong, and I owed her an apology for my assumptions and (over)reactions.

And apologize is exactly what I did. I looked her in the eye and told her how sorry I was. It used to be hard for me to own my mistakes, but if motherhood has taught me anything, it's that I make mistakes by the minute. I'm not fooling anyone with a guise of infallibility, nor do I want to. My daughter showed me a whole lot of grace when I apologized to her, and the next time she made a mistake, she was pretty quick to own it, too—and I was quick to accept it, to accept her. When we model accountability for our kids, they're more likely to mirror it. Modeling (always) speaks louder than telling.

Teaching our kids to show accountability online follows the same "lesson plan" as teaching them to apologize in person. Have a direct conversation, then follow it up regularly with shared examples. Listening, hearing, apologizing, accepting—these are the examples of online accountability we should model and share.

One of my favorite articles I've written is "6 Things Introverted Women Do Right" on *The Huffington Post*. I think introversion is better understood today and as a tried-and-true introvert, I'm grateful for that. I love to push the conversation away from what we can change about the introverts we know and love to how we can better understand what makes them tick.

When this article was shared widely, I wondered if there would be any negative reactions to it. With over one hundred comments on the site itself, only one sounded negative to me. A reader wrote that she thought introverts are selfish. Another reader jumped in and put her down for her thoughts.

When the first reader came back to explain herself (she meant selfish with their time, a coveted skill by many), the second reader circled back with something along the lines of, "I hear you." They had a dialogue and better understood each other because of it. This happened because they were both willing to step away from the defense line and toward each other.

Example: Online Disagreements

Show your kids what happens on your page as an example, or use these copycat examples and discuss what's going right in these dialogues and what's going wrong.

 Mark Sheridan This movie is stupid. The directors & writers should go jump off a bridge!

 Theresa Sapinsky Shut up, Mark! You're dumb and your opinion doesn't matter.

 Rahul Chaudry Mark, I agree that the movie was not well written, but that doesn't mean it shouldn't have been made.

 Theresa Sapinsky Mark has no idea what good movies are. Stupid people like him need to go jump off bridges, not the directors!

 Mark Sheridan Only an idiot can watch this and like it.

 Theresa Sapinsky Wow Mark ... that's insensitive.

GALIT BREEN

 Theresa Sapinsky God, why can't people learn to control their kids in public. If they were my kid, I'd put them over my knee right in front of everybody!

 Mark Sheridan Spanking is harmful to kids. I don't hit my kids.

 Theresa Sapinsky Mike, spaking is good for kids. My parents spanked me and I turned out great. Everybody should spank their kids when they misbehave.

 Rahul Chaudry My parents took a mixed approach. I only g⟨ spanked when I really deserved it--like when I did something serious.

 Mark Sheridan Theresa, unless you have research to back up your ridiculous theory, please don't open your fat mouth. Thx

 Mark Sheridan Who would want such a fat woman?? Gross!

 Theresa Sapinsky Good for this magazine for showing a plus-size woman on their ad!

 Rahul Chaudry Big women are gorgeous!

Discuss with Your Peers

This is one of those circus/monkeys situations.

We are responsible for monitoring the dialogue that happens in our own spaces. So if one of our friends is leaving rude comments on a picture or a status or a post that's ours, it's our responsibility to set the tone, model the good behavior, speak up, and delete only if necessary.

But we also need to maneuver trickier topics with our peers. How will we disagree on someone else's thread? And how will we share with each other if we see our kids disagreeing in ways that do more harm than good? These are all topics we can discuss with our parenting peers.

3 Takeaways:

- Engage in conversations, debates, discussions, and disagreements with the purpose of doing as much listening as talking.
- Only speak up if you have something to say. *Is what I'm about to say true, necessary, and kind?*
- When you're engaging in tricky conversations, don't be afraid to say, "I don't know," "I don't understand," and "I'm listening."

Chapter 8

The Internet Isn't Permanent, but It Is Public and It Is Loud

"I think [technology has] brought the world a lot closer together, and will continue to do that. There are downsides to everything; there are unintended consequences to everything."
— Steve Jobs

I'm a freelance writer for several magazines and websites. Sometimes I write personal essays and research-based articles. And, sometimes, I write product blurbs. Short, pithy paragraphs meant to describe—and sell—products.

I usually don't get to pick which products I write about. It's a surprise each time I get an assignment. Sometimes the surprise is pleasant and I get to write about what I know— like books, toys, and coffee. And, other times, it's not. I've written about vending machines, irons, and men's underwear.

When I got the underwear assignment, I burst out laughing. How could I not? I also did what one does, and I texted Jason photos of the underwear—tuxedo underwear, Halloween underwear, and sports-themed underwear. Sharing moments from our days makes the stretch from good-morning kisses to good-night exhaustion seem a little bit shorter.

What I didn't know when I sent those texts was that Jason was in the middle of a meeting. What I also didn't know was that he was using his phone during the meeting. And the other important thing I didn't know was that his peers were using his phone as well. Jason and his colleagues were on a conference call, sitting around a table, all eyes on his phone, which they were using to speak with the rest of their team members who weren't on-site.

And what did they all see pop up onto the screen in the middle of their meeting? Underwear.

Let's recap: tuxedo underwear, Halloween underwear, and sports-themed underwear. All the underwear.

While my messages were definitely seen by more people than I intended, no real harm was done. Luckily, Jason knew the people he was with well enough to quickly type "In a meeting" into his phone, and they could all laugh about the silliness of the moment.

He closed out our texts and my mistake was closed out with it.

We tend to use this kind of thinking about mistakes made on social media. One of the things that I've heard people say is that what happens on social media isn't actually permanent. Texts can be closed, photos can be deleted, statuses can be canceled, and just like that, mistakes disappear. This isn't always the case.

In 2006, Abercrombie & Fitch's CEO, Mike Jeffries, was quoted saying his brand doesn't sell pants for women larger than a size 10. The article included analysis reporting the company only wants "thin and beautiful people shopping in its store." Jeffries was quoted as saying A&F markets to "the cool kids." "Are we exclusionary?" he asked (himself). "Absolutely," he answered (to an unfortunate millions).

Seven years later, these words came back to haunt A&F. Bloggers, producers, and celebrities spoke out against their practices and many publicly announced they'd no longer shop at A&F. When things go viral, they take on a life of their own. Even if the original article had been deleted, it was spun, tweeted, and written about so many times, even Buzzfeed and Ellen DeGeneres criticized the company. In the words of the *Washington Post* writer Jena McGregor, "On the Internet, words never die."

The façade of the delete button seems to give people the leeway, freedom, and—in this case—unfortunate confidence to write, type, and post with wild abandon.

The problem is that people are in their own homes (or meetings!) and on their own devices independently of us, so we don't actually know who's online when we are, or who's seeing our mistakes before we reconsider the wisdom of posting that body shot, mean comment, or aggressive argument—and at any time, anyone can decide to capture our posts.

When I saved the negative comments about my weight on the article I wrote about marriage, I knew I was going to write about them. Even if those specific commenters had had a change of heart and decided to return to the thread and delete their words, it was too late. I'd already screencapped them, and when I included them in my article, they were seen by millions of people on *xoJane.com*, *TIME.com*, *Upworthy.com*, the *Today* show, and *Inside Edition*.

Our posts aren't permanent on our own feeds. But they can be captured and shared with so many more people than we ever intended. And that's what I mean when I say that the Internet is loud.

Snapchat is a platform that was created to solve this problem. Users can send photos and messages and set a time limit, one to ten seconds, that the message will stay live. After that time lapses, the message self-destructs.

But you know what doesn't self-destruct? Screencaps and recordings—even ones made from videos created on Snapchat.

In one case, Minnesotan father Bradley Knudson used his phone to record his fourteen-year-old daughter's bullies saying horrid things to her via Snapchat. He used the opportunity—and the evidence—to privately contact the girls' parents so they could discuss the problem. After several unreturned phone calls, one of the fathers responded by leaving his own hateful words on Knudson's voicemail. In a brilliant sign-of-the-times move, Knudson recorded this message and posted the whole story, names included, on YouTube. To date, his video has been viewed more than seven million times and the father who left the hateful messages was fired from his job.

In a different twist on the same vein, Jon Ronson wrote a fascinating article for the *New York Times Magazine* titled "How One Stupid Tweet Blew Up Justine Sacco's Life," in which he followed up with several regular, everyday people who had tweeted or shared something that they thought was harmless but went viral in a bad way. The people Ronson talked to were harassed in person and online, fired from their jobs, and in some cases isolated from their friends and family because of misconstrued social shares that were, more often than not, taken out of context. I love his angle of seeing things from someone else's point of view

GALIT BREEN

—there's a person on the other side of every share and every pink slip.

But I see a difference in purpose and intent between Ronson's examples and Knudson's actions. The people Ronson wrote about went from writing 140 characters on Twitter straight to being harassed with the purpose of shaming them for their tweet. I think that Knudson took the exact right steps in his situation. He tried to speak directly to his daughter's bullies' parents; when this tactic repeatedly failed and he was harassed in response to his attempts, he used technology and social media to create change. Members of one of the families whose daughter was involved in the bullying have apologized. Knudson's own family and community have engaged in important conversations. The school district is considering revamping their bullying prevention education program. So much happened as a result of a ten-second Snapchat conversation that was recorded.

People have been fired from jobs, grounded, and ostracized by friends in response to their shares on social media. We need to help our kids think twice before posting and realize that once they post something it is, indeed, permanent.

1 Resource:
"The Day My Blog Ruined My Life" by Jill Pond on *BlogHer.com* is an eye-opening, painfully truthful account of an adult who tweeted and blogged about people in her community—including kids and friends—and as a result became the topic of local gossip, lost a friendship, and was asked to not return to her kids' school to volunteer for a little while, until things "cooled down." She owned up to her mistakes and apologized profusely for them, and I actually

think she could have been given a little more slack. However, her story is real and common, and a great example of how quickly things can flip from a 140-character tweet to being life-changingly out of hand.

2 Things to Talk About:

Discuss with Your Kids

Sit down with your kids and show them how easy it is to capture someone else's post and have access to it even if the original post is deleted. Use the examples in this chapter or post something of your own, capture it, delete the original, and show how the capture is still there, with all of the sharing possibilities literally at your fingertips.

You may also want to discuss the fact that photos can be misused by people. This can—and does—happen. People who share photos of young children have found them in awful places and in awful hands. How much do your kids already know about topics like this? How much do you want them to know?

The mantras to teach (and reteach) here are: post like everyone's watching, assume what you post is permanent, and recognize that not everything needs to be posted.

When I first started using Facebook, I reconnected with childhood and college friends. I'd just stopped teaching, so I also used the platform to stay in touch with my former colleagues.

I was fully immersed in motherhood and parenting and I documented absolutely everything, from birthday parties to trips to museums, restaurants, and apple orchards.

Several years later, a writer friend had an article go viral. Another site reposted her writing without permission and swiped and published several of her old, personal Facebook photos to go along with it.

This was a reminder to me to rethink the wisdom of having so many photos of my own kids and family available online. Where I used to post albums, I now post photos, and I always think twice before I even do that.

Not everything needs to be documented and shared. What we all deem share-worthy will differ. But the thoughtfulness before we share should be consistent.

Discuss with Your Peers

If we see our friends posting something they might regret, we can give them a gentle nudge about how very loud and public and sharable the Internet is. Friends have done this for me.

When one of my kids was really little, I took a post-bath photo of them toddling away from me just after they had left their towel pooled at my feet. It was an in-the-thick-of-things slice of time when this harried, fleeting life of ours slowed down just for an instant. I could practically hear *childhood* whispered through my camera's click, and I was so very glad that I'd captured the moment.

When I posted the photo to Facebook, I got mostly what I bargained for. Likes and *Awws* in spades. But one of my friends sent me a private message questioning my decision to post a photo like this. At first blush, I was angry with her for taking something I thought was so sweet and making it anything but.

Digging a little bit deeper, I also know that my anger with her stemmed from embarrassment over making a possibly bad, and obviously visible, mistake.

I decided to ask several friends what they thought. I chose people like me who found lifelines on social media. If

I'm being truly honest, I probably knew these specific people would see things my way, which is why I cherry-picked them. They didn't disappoint. Each and every one gave me the reassurance I craved.

But after a few days, and many, many conversations about it, I ended up removing the photo. I came to the realization that if my friend thought posting the photo was in poor taste, there was a very good chance that someone else would think so, too.

I've never regretted that decision, and today I would never post any type of naked photos of my children. I'd be devastated if this kind of photo got into the wrong hands. My friend did me a favor.

I understand how difficult this can feel. But if we flip the script and remember that when we do this we're helping and protecting our friends, it can feel more palatable. We don't want anyone to be embarrassed, ridiculed, or hurt. We're all in this together.

I want to share with you another example of a time when I needed help and someone graciously gave it to me.

Sometimes it can be hard to remember that social media provides only slices of lives and experiences and moments. Our friends' shares work like jumbled puzzle pieces; pretty and shiny and click-worthy, but not necessarily whole stories. And that's what this example illuminates—a time when I forgot to look into the background, or context, of a friend's post before I commented on it.

One evening I was scrolling, "liking," and commenting, when I was struck by a stunning photo. A far-away friend had posted a picture of a beautiful baby and it immediately caught my eye. The lighting. The cheeks. The hipster hat. "Dying," I commented. *Of cuteness*, I meant. And I kept scrolling.

Later that night I was lying in bed reading or Instagramming or pinning, probably trying to convince myself that it was time to go to bed, when a message from that friend popped up onto my screen.

Don't give it a second thought … Just seeing the word "dying" will jolt her … I know you'd never want to cause a mom an ounce of pain … Bits and pieces of my friend's message showed and I will admit that I was confused. What could possibly have gone wrong with my comment? Such a cute baby, such a cute picture.

When I clicked through, I saw the whole story. My friend had posted the photo in honor of a fellow mama whose heart was hurting because her beautiful baby was diagnosed with a very long, rocky road. To her, my comment "Dying" would conjure anything but *of cuteness.*

My friend did the absolute right thing by deleting my comment and reaching out to me to tell me why. This was her circus. She was protecting her friend's heart, and she was teaching me about looking into the whole story before commenting.

She handled it so gracefully and she was 100 percent right. I would never want to hurt anyone, and I was very grateful to be told and helped.

If you're in my friend's position, try taking this standpoint. You're the helper, and most people do want to be helped and would never want to be the one doing the hurting.

And if you're on the receiving end of this help, take it.

The phenomenon of commenting before reading the whole story isn't new. Online perusers are known for taking single lines from posts, articles, and even introductions, titles, and photos and nitpicking the minutiae within them until they fray. We all have to remember, and to teach our kids, that if we don't have the time or the interest to look into the whole issue, or read the whole article, and form and articulate a thoughtful response or question, then we don't get to engage.

We look for positives. We comment thoughtfully. We seek to understand. And that is all.

3 Takeaways:

- Everything you share has the potential to be seen by an exponentially bigger number of people than you imagine. Post like everyone is watching.
- Deleting something doesn't necessarily make it go away, so think before you post.
- Not everything needs to be said or shared.

Chapter 9

Just Because You See It, Doesn't Mean It's Yours

"I try to make good decisions as decisions come up."
— Ashton Kutcher

The last chapter was about being mindful of not posting things online that you don't want others to misuse. This section is about making sure that you're not the one misusing someone else's posts.

I want to discuss an aspect of my viral *xoJane.com* article that falls into this fuzzy area of screencapping and using what's not yours. Because fuzzy is exactly what it is.

I wrote that article purposefully. When the comments about my weight came through on my article about marriage on *The Huffington Post*, I was devastated and humiliated. I went back and looked at them more times than I care to admit. I'm not sure I can explain why I did that.

Maybe I was hoping they would go away or that someone would tell those commenters to knock it off. Neither one of these things happened, so as Lily Tomlin said, I realized that I was someone and I could be the one to do something.

I screencapped and saved the comments on my desktop until I could move away from a sad place to a more productive one and write about the situation.

The comments I saved were not my words and not on my own Facebook page. But they were about me, so I used them as if they were my own.

I'm fully aware that there's a fuzziness to this. From my perspective, I was telling my own story and calling out the bullies in it. When discussing this, I often deferred to author Anne Lamott, who wisely said, "If you wanted to be portrayed better, you should have acted better."

But there were definitely people who thought I should have blocked out the names and pictures from the unkind comments before I shared them.

While I don't regret what I did, I can definitely see the other side—and I think the discussion around this issue is valuable. Intention is key. In this case, mine was to open a dialogue about body talk and cyberbullying.

Before I shared those commenters' names and photos, I thought about it. My editors, who could have vetoed this decision, thought about it, too. When I share something that isn't mine, as I did in this case, I've made it a habit to ask myself why I'm sharing it. If it's not for a good reason, then I don't do it.

The caveat to doing this is realizing not everyone will agree with you on what a "good" reason is. We have to be okay with this and be open to the conversation if someone disagrees with us. We also need to be open to being the one to start the same kind of conversation with others.

Another good practice is to ask for permission before using other people's photos, ideas, or words. If you don't feel comfortable asking, the answer to whether or not you should use it might be clarified.

GALIT BREEN

Writer Caitlin Seida wrote a compelling article related to this issue called "My Embarrassing Picture Went Viral" on *Salon.com*. In it, she chronicled her experience of having a Halloween photo she shared of herself in costume as Lara Croft, Tomb Raider, go viral on platforms such as Twitter, Tumblr, Reddit, 9GAG, and FAIL Blog, with the words "Fridge Raider" written across it. Her words perfectly address the need to remember that there's always someone on the other side of your online actions and that if something isn't yours, it's also not yours to share.

Her experience is an interesting one to juxtapose against mine when discussing purpose and intent. I see a difference between sharing the comments written about me and sharing Seida's photo. You might not. Agreeing to disagree here is okay. The gold, and the learning, lie in the thinking and the conversation.

1 Resource:
"You Might Want to Watermark Photos of Your Children" by Maria Mora on *SheKnows.com* is a startling look at how people take things online that aren't theirs. This writer shared a photo of her infant son and years later still finds it used on hundreds of websites and even sold as Etsy prints —all without her permission. This is eerily easy to do.

2 Things to Talk About:

Discuss with Your Kids
Sit down with your kids and scroll through your feed, their feed, or their friends' feeds and discuss what it would look like to share someone else's words and photos.

We need to talk about what's okay to share and what's not, what requires asking the other person for permission, and what's just fine to share without asking for consent.

Discuss intent. It's key here.

We've already discussed the "games" kids play on Instagram, such as tagging who you want "out" and "matchmaking" unknowing peers. In both of these kinds of posts, kids' photos are reposted without permission. Do kids have a right to do this? Why or why not? This is perfect fodder for short discussions and interesting dialogue.

In these cases we don't have to agree—with each other or even with our kids—on what's right and what's not. I'd guess the answers fall into the "fuzzy" gray area category. But even without a definitive answer, the discussions we'll have about this topic will hopefully lead to thoughtful decision making, and that makes them so very worthwhile.

Discuss with Your Peers
We can have similar discussions with our peers. If we see someone sharing something that's clearly not theirs, we can talk to them about it, send them a private message, or give them a gentle nudge.

People who write online often express their opinions within comment threads. You and I can do this as well. We just need to remember how to disagree thoughtfully.

When I was taking education courses toward earning my master's degree, I had a wonderful professor who said to always approach teaching something hard as if the other person authentically doesn't know how to do it.

Assume that the person you're talking to doesn't know that it's not okay to use someone else's photo, not that they're doing so to purposefully do something wrong. You're helping, remember?

3 Takeaways:

- Just because you see it on the Internet doesn't mean it's yours.

- Ask for permission before posting something that isn't yours. If you don't feel comfortable asking, then really consider why that is before posting.

- Before you share a photo of someone else, consider your intent. Make sure the way and reason you're sharing it is true, necessary, and kind.

Chapter 10

Anonymous Isn't an Excuse: You're Responsible for Every Word You Write Online

"I've always told Will, 'You can do whatever you want as long as you can look at yourself in the mirror and be okay.'"
— Jada Pinkett Smith

I write early in the morning. It's usually still dark out when I make my way downstairs. My writing nook is small but my desk chair is big and cozy and has garish yellow flowers on it. I love it.

This is where I was sitting and trying to think of an example of someone doing the right thing when no one was watching. But the whole point of doing something like that is that no one knows what you did! So I was having a hard time coming up with one.

As I was combing through my memories, my daughter came downstairs.

She's always the first one up and once she is, she's ready for the day. Clothes on, hair brushed, brain swirling. I had one of these three going for me when she slipped into my lap.

"What are you working on?" she asked. I smoothed her hair away from her face, kissed her cheek, and asked if she could come up with an example. She didn't fail me.

She thought for a single heartbeat, then started listing her examples, ticking each one on her fingertips.

When your mom makes peanut butter cookies and leaves them out and you go fill up your water bottle and you don't take even one. (Guess what I had made the night before?)

When someone in your class gets new mechanical pencils and you have plain pencils and they leave one of their pencils laying out by the lockers and you pick it up and give it back to them.

When your brother asks you to trade a dollar for a quarter because he just **doesn't know** *and you explain it to him.*

As she went on and on I thought, *Oh yes, this is exactly how it is.* Life is a series of choices. We purposefully choose to make the right ones—the ones that don't do any harm—because it's the right thing to do and because that's the kind of person we want to be.

And while it might be hard to come up with examples of other people doing the right thing unobserved (because that's the whole point!), it's not hard to pinpoint how it feels to be on the receiving end of anonymous kind and unkind behavior.

We all make mistakes; of course we do. But a mistake is different from using the fact that no one is looking, the fact that you're logged in as Anonymous, as an opportunity to do the wrong thing.

When commenters said unkind things about me online, a lot of people gave me a knowing look and a nod and said things like, "It's because they're anonymous," which absolutely blew my mind.

Anonymity isn't an excuse to do harm. Not ever.

On the flip side of this experience, I was shown a tremendous amount of kindness. So many people reached out to me in support and solidarity. Some did so via e-mails and others via comments. Some of them were even anonymous. These people grasped an opportunity to lift me up. I knew it when I saw and felt it, because I've been on the receiving end of kindness ripples before.

My second year of teaching was my first year living in Minnesota. When I visited Jason while we were dating long-distance the year before, the winter weather was an aberration—70 degrees in February. Jason looked dubious at both my "I've got this" proclamations and the corduroy jacket I deemed a winter coat. More than a decade of Minnesota winters later, I can confidently say that I definitely do not have winters under control. Now when the snow starts falling, sometimes as early as Halloween, my proclamations sound more like, "I'm new here."

But that first year was definitely the worst. What softened and warmed that winter was that I worked at a lovely school with a supportive staff, and the class I had was pure lovely. One afternoon I trudged to my car after a full day of work and snow to find someone had scraped the windshield for me. Another cold morning, there was a latte sitting on my desk when I got to school. On my February birthday, someone left potted plants on my bookshelf, hoping this would make it feel more like spring.

Mary Fisher of *100GoodDeeds.org* defines a good deed as, "a time we've gone out of our way to help someone and [it] only counts if the deed remains anonymous."

When it comes to online kindness, we can mold and meld this definition to say *still counts* if you're anonymous—or if you're logged in as Anonymous.

You can do a whole lot of harm or a whole lot of good with anonymity. Each time you post is an opportunity to land on the right side of kindness. Keep making the right choice every time you get this chance.

1 Resource:

"Having the Sex Talk with a Teenage Boy" by Mackenzie Siders on *ScaryMommy.com* is a personal essay describing the smart and important way one mom addressed sex and using protection with her teenage son. My favorite part of what she wrote, besides the fact that she addressed this potentially uncomfortable conversation directly, is that she said that once she had these conversations, she was able to stop worrying about her son and the first time he chose to have sex—because she'd prepared him the best ways she could. Discussing the facets of acting kindly online isn't different from this. We need to teach our kids to be accountable and ready in real life and online.

2 Things to Talk About:

Discuss with Your Kids

I've started every single one of these sections with, "Sit down with your kids … " That was on purpose. We absolutely cannot hand our kids phones and Instagram passwords and tell them to go to town, patting ourselves on the back for a milestone met.

I'm not worried about how old your kids are when they get a phone or an account on any social media platform. There are age restrictions on all of these accounts. You'll have to decide for yourself what these mean for you and your family.

But there's a danger in adhering to these age guidelines without thought, and that's what I am worried about.

Once we're ready, comfortable, and have the time to discuss the accountability of our online actions, the ripples we create with them, and the impact of posting anonymously, we're ready to parent a kid who's online.

We need to take the time—to sit down, so to speak—to have these discussions repeatedly and transparently, because we're all responsible for every single thing we post.

Discuss with Your Peers

"I did then what I knew how to do. Now that I know better, I do better."
– Maya Angelou

Now we know better, so let's do better, and let's do so together.

The challenge in conversing with our peers about online kindness is matching the openness we create in conversations with our kids. This can feel daunting. The secret to overcoming this is sharing our own worries and mistakes.

When we let our guard down and share the less shiny parts of our parenting, what we're really doing is letting others in.

When I texted a friend that I felt horrid about yelling at my daughter for misplacing her gloves, she told me we'd be okay. Then she shared her own experiences and encouraged me to apologize. While I'd started off the morning feeling frustrated, discouraged, and alone, after chatting with her I felt supported, sane, and armed with a

117

plan to fix things with my daughter this time and to do things better next time.

I've had this experience online as well. One of the first posts I ever published on my blog was about a spilled smoothie. Actually, it was about forgetting to put the top on a blender while making a smoothie and drenching everything in sight, white T-shirt and small children included, with blueberry smoothie remnants. I wrote about how I instantly turned on myself, saying awful words in my mind; I was self-talking in a way that wasn't healthy.

I worried how this post would make me appear and how it would be received. But my readers—not yet friends, as I was too new to blogging at the time—responded with gentle kindness. Many also responded by saying, "Me, too."

While most of my readers probably hadn't forgotten to place the tops on their blenders before pressing *On*, they all absolutely knew what it feels like to make a mistake.

The same is true as we make decisions about when, or whether, our kids may be online, and how we'll choose to help them when they make mistakes. The details may differ, but we can all relate to the similarities we'll find in the experiences of learning and fumbling and learning some more.

The first time my daughter seriously asked for an Instagram account, I took the question to Facebook to see what other parents were thinking and doing about their kids and social media use. We didn't need to leave the conversation in solidarity that all of our tweens could or could not have accounts. That wasn't the goal of my post. What I was looking for—and found—was a chance to engage in a thoughtful dialogue and to find out why some parents gave a firm *no* in this decision and some said *yes*.

Within this kind of unguarded sharing and dialogue, without any pressure to be right, it feels safer to be accountable for our choices and actions. This means making good decisions as they come up, apologizing for mistakes when they inevitably arise, and accepting others' apologies, as the same trial-and-error process applies to them as well. You might not ever have the experience of knowing that a friend is being unkind anonymously online. Only one friend of mine has ever admitted to recognizing that another friend was writing negative anonymous comments in a blog thread. She took a chance and wrote her friend a private message asking if it was her and if she wanted to talk. This was brave and bold and a very unique situation. More than likely, the conversations you have with your peers will be about how to best teach kids to be accountable for their online actions.

We're all learning. We can all always do better. And we can—and should—all hold each other responsible for our online behavior, and help each other ensure that kindness wins.

3 Takeaways:

- No excuses. If we're being unkind, even anonymously, it's still on us. We're in the wrong.
- If we make a mistake, we need to be accountable and apologize for it (and try not to do it again).
- Kindness wins. Always.

Parent-to-Parent Kindness Wins Contract

"As you navigate through the rest of your life, be open to collaboration. Other people and other people's ideas are often better than your own. Find a group of people who challenge and inspire you, spend a lot of time with them, and it will change your life."
— Amy Poehler

The hard, time-consuming tasks of talking about and revisiting how to act kindly online are, by far, our most important work.

So first of all, I want to thank you with every fiber of my being for getting to this part with me. This is where we all agree to not just want kindness to win, but to be the ones who make sure that it does.

Reading this book will help with this. But using your own words and having your own conversations is the leap. *You* are what will make the biggest difference.

The conversations about online kindness we'll have with our kids are where the golden sparkles of change can shine. Education is our path there. But it's the conversations we'll have with our peers that have the potential to be platinum.

There's really only one thing I want you to promise your friends, and this is it: take care of each other and each other's kids.

Earlier in the book, I stated that the only time it's worth causing a kerfuffle with a peer about his or her online behavior is when their actions hurt my kids or me. What would happen if we all agreed to intentionally swap every "my" with an "our"?

Our problems, our kids, our education, our solutions, our change. We'll all do and be better in working toward this together.

If we agree to watch out for each other, to help each other, and to remember that all of us and our children are learning and we need all the help we can get, then this big job of expecting, teaching, and advocating for online kindness will suddenly become more bite-sized, easier to maneuver, and a whole lot more manageable.

When my daughter first joined Instagram, the older girls she knew from sports and family ties immediately took to her side, gently showing her the (social media) ropes. Kids and teens often seem wildly instinctive, following their gut feelings and emotions in ways that are unpredictable and often uncomfortable to witness. Goodness knows that there's so much to learn from time and experience, but maybe in this case, our instinct-following kids are on to something. We should instinctively take care of each other.

So what I'm asking of you is to be the one who takes the first step in reaching out to the mom or dad sitting next to you—even if their kid was mean to yours or your kid was unkind to theirs—and approach them like you both know that we're all in this together, that kindness wins when there's an *us*.

And if someone else takes the first step toward you, then I'm asking you to grab hold of them tightly. They're a keeper friend and someone you want to have close.

This is why I'm closing this section with a Parents of Tweens and Teens Manifesto. Ten *I wills* that have nothing and everything to do with our kids. "Nothing" because these points are focused on how we'll treat other parents we know who have kids in a similar life stage as ours. And "everything" because when we choose to be on the same team, everyone and everything wins, kindness included.

You can share this contract, this manifesto, with your friends or keep it tucked away as a personal mission statement committing to kindness. Both ways are perfect and effective and right.

The Parents of Tweens and Teens Manifesto

I will remember that we're all learning.

I will tell you what I learn.

I will listen when you tell me what you know.

I will look out for your child like I do my own.

I will work with you to make sure that both of our kids are in a safe, kind online space.

I will admit when I'm wrong.

I will show you grace when you admit the same.

I will hold my kids accountable for being kind to yours.

I will remember that your kids are good as they're learning the same.

I will know—and act like I know—that we're in this together.

Signature: _____

Signature: _____

Parent-to-Child Kindness Wins Contract

"I think we need more love in the world. We need more kindness, more compassion, more joy, more laughter. I definitely want to contribute to that."
— Ellen DeGeneres

At first blush, having these conversations with our kids can seem daunting. But realizing that we can help our kids be the ones who bring goodness and kindness to those around them makes it all seem so ridiculously worth it.

No matter where you and your kids are with social media use, whether you've just started or aren't quite there, I'm gently suggesting that you can begin anywhere. Any part of the dialogue around online kindness is a perfect starting point. One small conversation at a time is all we need to begin building the concept of online kindness as a norm, as an expectation.

Some of your kids might already be online, and you might have that sinking feeling in your tummy that it's too late, they're already there, and the mess of untangling any misinformation they have about how to act kindly online will work itself out. But if there's one thing I've learned as a teacher, as a parent, and as a human being, it's that it's never too late to learn and to do better.

When I was a classroom teacher, I heard an amazing speaker talk about newness and change in education and how we were absolutely responsible for being informed about both.

He said: *What if you decided to have eye surgery, and when you went in for your appointment, your doctor said that he knows there are new ways to do the surgery, but he was trained in doing it with steel surgical blades. This technique worked for many people and he already has a box of these blades in the supply closet so he might as well use them. So that new technology that uses lasers and is less painful, more effective, and faster? Naah. He's not going to use that.*

You wouldn't stand for this, would you? Actually, you might stand up and run away! Well, it's the exact same thing with teaching, parenting, and learning.

You're right where you need to be—ready and willing to learn and to create change.

So I'm ending this section by arming you with one more tool in our fight for online kindness—a *Kindness Wins* contract to share with your kids.

The perfect recipe for teaching just about anything includes a short, direct lesson followed by repeated examples, discussions, and opportunities to try our best, make mistakes, and try again. This contract includes the essence of the short, direct "lessons" you'll teach, in no particular order. Begin anywhere.

Kindness Wins Contract

1. Before you post, ask yourself if what you're about to share is kind, necessary, and true.

2. Consider your post's intent and think about other people's perspectives and feelings.

3. Get permission before posting something that isn't yours. If you don't feel comfortable asking, figure out why that is before you post it.

4. Practice the words you'll say to stand up against unkind online actions.

5. The way you present yourself online should mirror the way you present yourself in person.

6. Use your "like" currency kindly. Drop love bombs whenever possible.

7. No body talk, no body photos.

8. Debate issues, not people.

9. Post as if everyone is watching.

10. If you wouldn't post something with your name attached to it, then don't post it at all.

11. Remember that not everything needs to be posted.

12. Be kind. Always.

Adult Signature: _____

Child Signature: _____

Conclusion

"Telling a story in a futuristic world gives you this freedom to explore things that bother you in contemporary times."
— Suzanne Collins

After reading ten chapters filled with worries laced with calls for kindness, you might be feeling that you need to be anxious about letting your kids have access to social media.

I want you to know that this couldn't possibly be further from the truth.

As someone who's experienced firsthand the goodness so easily found on social media, including friendships, career opportunities, and a ridiculous number of life lessons, I can confidently declare my love for it. Social media brings people together. It allows us to share our thoughts and our moments. We're able to be creative in our posts and share things that are important and meaningful with the people who matter to us. It's also the great equalizer between extroverts and introverts —everyone has a voice online.

My work and my fun often intermix on social media. I'm beyond excited to share this passion with my children, and I hope you feel the same way about sharing online spaces with your kids. My goal in writing this book is to encourage us all to do this thoughtfully.

This means doing so in a way that works for your family. At our house, this doesn't mean waiting until our children hit the age requirement stated on each site. It means waiting until each one reaches the maturity level—and Jason and I reach the bandwidth—to engage in ongoing discussions about how to act kindly while they're online.

I'm actually an advocate of starting these tricky conversations with our kids when they're a little bit younger and a little bit more open to our parenting opinions. At a certain point the meaningfulness scale will edge away from us and toward their friends. I wonder if the right time to teach online kindness is while it's still tipping in our favor.

So I'm adding online kindness to the long list of tough topics that are my privilege to discuss with my kids— friendships, relationships, periods, sex, sexuality, alcohol, drugs, voting, religion, and how to maneuver kindly online.

You might not agree with everything I wrote in these pages. And that's okay. We don't have to—and probably shouldn't—parent our kids in the exact same way, because every family is different. The only thing we all do need to do in the same way is to agree to talk to our kids about online kindness.

I believe with every fiber of my being that there can't be change without discourse. So thank you for being a conversation-starter and a change-maker.

RESOURCES

"I don't think we should see the world of books as fundamentally separate from the world of the Internet. Yes, the Internet contains a lot of videos of squirrels riding skateboards, but it can also be a place that facilitates big conversations."
— John Green

"Should We Talk to Young Children about Race?" by Rodolfo Mendoza-Denton on GreaterGood.com

Nurture Shock by Po Bronson and Ashley Merryman

"The Secret Language of Girls on Instagram" by Rachel Simmons on Time.com

"The One Conversation That Could Save Your Teen's Life (and Your Own)" by Glennon Doyle Melton on Momastery.com

"Parenting as a Gen Xer: We're the First Generation of Parents in the Age of iEverything" by Allison Slater Tate on WashingtonPost.com

"I Wrote an Article about Marriage, and All Anyone Noticed Is That I'm Fat," by Galit Breen on xoJane.com

"A Letter to My Daughters about Weed" by Dan Shapiro on Open.Salon.com

"How to Take a Screenshot on an iPhone or iPod Touch" by Brandon Widder on DigitalTrends.com

"Rude Reactions, Angry Outbursts, and Ladders That Lift" by Rachel Macy Stafford on HandsFreeMama.com

"6 Things Introverted Women Do Right" by Galit Breen on HuffingtonPost.com

"Abercrombie & Fitch's Big, Bad Brand Mistake" by Jena McGregor on WashingtonPost.com

"Racism and Bullying in Prior Lake, Minnesota" by Bradley Knudson on YouTube.com

"How One Stupid Tweet Blew Up Justine Sacco's Life" by Jon Ronson on NewYorkTimes.com

"The Day My Blog Ruined My Life" by Jill Pond on BlogHer.com

"You Might Want to Watermark Photos of Your Children" by Maria Mora on SheKnows.com

"Having the Sex Talk with a Teenage Boy" by Mackenzie Siders on ScaryMommy.com

"My Embarrassing Picture Went Viral" by Caitlin Seida on Salon.com

"The History of Laser Vision Correction" on Lasik.com

100 Good Deeds founded by Mary Fisher

OUR FAVORITE PEANUT BUTTER COOKIES

"I wouldn't keep him around long if I didn't feed him
well."
— Julia Child

Minnesotans believe that you should never show up to
gatherings empty-handed and that all good conversations
happen over snacks. So here's our recipe for peanut butter
cookies—the ones that, when left sitting on the kitchen
counter, are hard but apparently possible for daughters to
resist.

Make the cookies; have the conversations.

Minnesota Peanut Butter Cookies

Ingredients:
1 cup peanut butter
1 cup sugar
1 teaspoon baking powder
1 egg, beaten

Directions:
1. Mix all of the ingredients together.

2. Roll the dough into cookie-sized small balls.

3. Bake the cookies at 325 degrees F on a prepared pan for
about 10 minutes.

Makes 3 dozen cookies

ACKNOWLEDGEMENTS

To my motherhood, blogging, and writing tribes— There are too many of you to list, and you know how angsty I get about inadvertently forgetting someone whom I adore (almost) as much as dark chocolate, but you know who you are. You're the people who taught me that a woman with a pen is powerful. And then you taught me to believe that I could be one of those women with a pen. I could be a woman with lots of pens, even. Everything that's right about my writing is because of you. ***Thank you.***

To my first book readers—Rachel Macy Stafford, who gave me every lift I needed and Katrina Kenison, whose voice I hear saying, "Do the hard work," every single time I sit down to write. Sherri Kuhn, Sheila McCraith, Kimberly McCreight, Sue Scheff, Jill Smokler, and Marcelle Soviero, who are the goodness I strive to be. The eight of you breathe truth into the mantra that, as women, we're meant to lift each other up. ***Thank you.***

To all those who helped me publish—Katherine Fye Sears, Jennifer Gilbert, Jesse James, Tricia Parker, and Adam Bodendieck, you are truly the best hand-holders a girl could ask for. ***Thank you.***

To my book manager, Pam Labbe—You gave me every push I needed, showed me that there's more than one way to do things, and kept your promise that I never have to do anything that makes my tummy hurt. ***Thank you.***

To my graphic designer, Rachel Mizer—Your creative prowess is inspiring, and you never disowned me for asking a million-bajillion questions. ***Thank you.***

To my editor, Bethany Root—You're a gift, and a brilliant one at that. You not only showed me how to make words sparkle, you also explained ambiguous-to-me grammar rules—slowly and repeatedly. ***Thank you.***

To Jason—You gave up several football-watching Sundays to give me time to write, to clink beers with me in celebration of chapters completed well and in anticipation of chapters that Bethany was sure to have me redo. Thank you for being my other half. *I choose you.*

To Brody—You said it was "really okay" that so much of our fleeting time together was spent writing side by side; thank you for that. *Keep telling your stories, I'm listening.*

To Chloe and Kayli—You were stunning early readers. Your thoughts and comments and questions were perfect reminders that our kids come to us shiny and it's our job to give them chances to stay that way. *Find your spark, let it shine.*

To Parker—Thank you for trading a few walks for naps. I needed those. *You're a wonderful writing partner.*

And to you, my new friend—Thank you for reading till the very end. Please find me at TheseLittleWaves.com. *Ohmygoodness, do I ever want to hear from you.*

About the Author

Galit Breen was a classroom and reading teacher for ten years. She has a master's degree in education and a bachelor's degree in human development. In 2009, she launched a career as a freelance writer entrenched in social media. Since then, her work has been featured in various online magazines including *Brain, Child, The Huffington Post, TIME,* and *xoJane.* She lives in Minnesota with her husband, three children, and a ridiculously spoiled miniature golden doodle. You can learn more about Galit by visiting TheseLittleWaves.com.

CPSIA information can be obtained
at www.ICGtesting.com
Printed in the USA
LVOW08s0040021116
511276LV00007B/231/P